S T E P H E N   W A S S

the amateur archaeologist

Taylor & Francis
Taylor & Francis Group

LONDON AND NEW YORK

To my mother and father

© Stephen Wass 1992

First published 1992

711 Third Avenue, New York, NY 10017
2 Park Square, Milton Park, Abingdon, Oxfordshire OX14 4RN

Typeset by Lasertext, Stretford, Manchester

Published by Taylor & Francis

First issued in paperback 2011

A CIP catalogue record for this book is
available from the British Library

ISBN13: 978-0-7134-6896-0 (hbk)
ISBN13: 978-0-4155-1541-2 (pbk)

Illustrations

Technical Note

Most of the photographs in this book were taken with a Minolta X
700. The line illustrations were drawn using MacDraw II by Claris
on an Apple Macintosh Classic and printed with an Apple
Stylewriter.

Contents

Acknowledgements

I would like to say a special thank you to Philip Rahtz both for the encouragement and advice he gave to a young 'digger' and for offering detailed comments on the text of this book. Many of the plans included in this volume were originally surveyed and drawn with an old friend Ralph Walker who now builds castles in his spare time, my thanks to him. As part of the 'Bordesley team' for many years I would like to thank Grenville Astill, Sue Wright, Sue Hirst, Iain McCaig and David Walsh for many hours of instruction and entertainment. Special thanks go to David Esplin and the Dorset Institute of Higher Education for allowing me access to material from his HND dissertation on Blashenwell Farm. Further thanks go to David for his help in supplying additional photographs and for the close interest he has taken in the preparation of this book. Thanks also to Alistair Marshall for allowing me to feature aspects of his work at Guiting Power. Photographs 5, 7, 15, 18a, 28, 37, 68 and 75 are by David Esplin; 14 is by Verna Wass; 36 by Bryan Martin; and 91 by Alistair Marshall.

Finally apologies to all those who appear willingly or unwillingly in the photographs in the book, I hope I caught your better sides.

Unless otherwise credited, all photographs were taken on site at Bordesley Abbey.

Foreword

Archaeology has become a popular subject, with a wide public interest in excavations, museums and heritage sites. In Britain the role of the amateur has been important in the development of the subject; but increasing professionalism and the rapid growth of high-tech archaeological science, obscure theory and computerization have in recent years tended to discourage the beginner from becoming involved.

There is, however, now a change, brought about partly by financial cut backs to professional archaeology, and partly by the increasing availability of people with leisure. Steve Wass's book is for those who want to get involved but are afraid of being inadequate, or of being rebuffed. Step-by-step he explains what archaeology is about and how anyone can participate. He does not underestimate the difficulties or the hardships that often accompany archaeology in the field. As an amateur digger of long experience he is well qualified to point the way to responsible involvement. Simple explanations and a reader-friendly style make this a useful guide for those who ask: how can I work in archaeology?

Philip Rahtz
Emeritus Professor
Department of Archaeology
University of York

Introduction

This book sets out to be a comprehensive and practical guide to developing an interest in archaeology. It turns out also to be a very personal book because it centres on an activity with which I have been closely associated for the past 25 years. It is personal because in writing it I call to mind many of the friends I have made and the enjoyment we have shared. The way the book unfolds reflects my own awakening interest in archaeology. My earliest archaeological memory was sitting on a beach in Devon with a favourite 'uncle'. The afternoon was hot and most of the family were dozing but we were playing a game. 'What's this?', I would demand waving a knotted piece of driftwood about. 'Ah, that's a dinosaur's backbone.' 'What about this?', an old tin lid this time. 'Now that's a piece of Roman soldier's armour.' And so it went on through the afternoon until the sun began to dip and the sands clear. What patience he must have had! Was this the awakening of a life-long interest?

1 A family holiday, visiting the Roman remains at Caerleon.

9

2 Midsummer Hill
Camp, a page from an
early notebook.

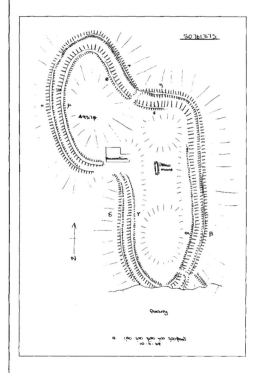

By the age of ten I was dragging my parents and baby brother
round every ancient monument I could find. As soon as a family
holiday was announced I would pore over a set of road maps and
identify the positions of likely antiquities (1). Nobody got anywhere
very quickly in an Austin A45 van and when there were continual
diversions to look at this castle or that abbey the journeys must have
been interminable. I inflicted these 'round about' trips on my family
for several years and then they bought me a bicycle.

We were living on the southern fringes of Birmingham at the time
and it was a long way to any of the places I knew about, Kenilworth
and Warwick Castles, Ragley Hall, Chedworth. Then one day,
during a geography lesson, one inch to the mile Ordnance Survey
maps were unfolded for the first time. As the symbols were explained
to us I began to realize that the whole countryside was thickly
spread with ancient monuments! At the HMSO bookshop in town
where I purchased my first one-inch map I also picked up *Field
Archaeology – Some notes for beginners issued by the Ordnance
Survey*. The first independent expedition, together with my friend

Ralph Walker, was on Saturday 11 March, 1967. We were fourteen at the time and spent the day cycling along the Roman Icknield Street to visit The Mount at Beoley. The very next day we were off to the Iron Age Camp on Wychbury Hill. For the next three years we travelled throughout central England recording, photographing and measuring all manner of earthworks (2).

Back at school Ralph and I founded the Archaeological Society. It only had a membership of two but that did not bother us. We were watched over by our president, a rather bemused classics master who one day, early in 1968, passed on to us a circular which had gone round local schools. Redditch Urban District Council were not only organizing a dig but they were offering payment at the rate of 7 s 6 d (37 pence) a day! The site was in a meadow north of the town where there were said to be the remains of an abbey. We were a little dubious at first but soon got to work stripping turf, after an hour or so we were taken off the job and sent down the valley to begin on 'the industrial site', where we continued to work for another ten days.

None of it made much sense but we picked up things as we went along. In all this I felt something of an outsider, never really sure of what was going on and reluctant to ask. Then everything changed. One Sunday afternoon we cycled out to revisit a small site marked on the map as Moons Moat (3). To our astonishment it was being excavated. A local teacher called Mike Wise and a colleague from London, Chris Medley were working with local volunteers to save the site from development. As 'old hands' in the digging game we

3   Moon's Moat, plan of the excavations.

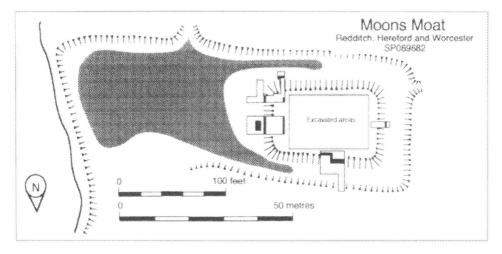

were welcomed with open arms and started working there most weekends. I was given an enormous amount of help and encouragement on the site and found myself supervising areas at the age of 16. This was all part of archaeological work centred on what was becoming Redditch new town. Excavations were springing up all over the place and I worked whenever and wherever I could throughout the early 1970s.

I had also kept my links with Bordesley and returned there when Philip Rahtz, then lecturing at the School of History at Birmingham University, took over. In my third season, Philip gave me the responsibility for completing the excavation of the boundary bank. I must have done a reasonably good job because I have been working in one capacity or another there ever since. In 1986 I had the enormous satisfaction of supervising the removal of an intact medieval timber tailrace to be conserved in the same workshop alongside timbers from the *Mary Rose* in Portsmouth (4). A difficult and demanding operation completed successfully, just 10 metres and 18 years away from my first picking up a trowel.

4 Bordesley Abbey industrial site, lifting the last timber from the earliest of the mill's tailraces.

1 *What is archaeology all about?*

In the public eye

Every now and then archaeology will hit the headlines, either because treasure has been unearthed and an expert opinion is quoted or because another chunk of the national heritage is about to be dug away. 'Call for law change after ruling on £20m treasure', introduces a piece on the Snettisham hoard of gold and silver ornaments while 'Troy Town under siege after divine intervention', leads into an article about the preservation of an ancient maze on the Scilly Isles. Being in the public eye at times of crisis creates a rather unbalanced view of archaeology which is compounded by the antics of the fictional archaeologist. By far the most eminent of these during the 1980s was Indiana Jones. He was an heroic figure who, armed only with a floppy hat and a bull-whip, saved western civilization. Most contemporary archaeologists have rather more modest ambitions; yet despite their attempts to hide behind theoretical frameworks and data files archaeology is still seen as a glamorous pastime.

In-depth news coverage is reserved for events which, irrespective of their archaeological importance, demand publicity by association. The help of a royal connection was demonstrated by the raising of Henry VIII's war ship, the *Mary Rose*. Shakespeare comes a close second making a walk on appearance at the site of the Rose Theatre on the south bank of the Thames. If contemporary personalities become involved, be it Prince Charles in a diving suit or Dustin Hoffman in a T-shirt, so much the better.

Archaeology is sometimes featured in magazines or on television programmes where again the focus will be on newsworthy events or people. Although there is no longer a media personality of the standing of Mortimer Wheeler others have made their mark. Occasionally there will be more extensive coverage of a theme such as the search for Troy or the archaeology of the Bible lands. Generally the accent is on the romance of distant places and remote times. Every now and then publicity will be given in the media to a major archaeological exhibition and crowds will come in their thousands to queue for hours to catch glimpses of gold in glass cases.

Many people still see local museums as dull places where collections of dusty pots shed their labels in an atmosphere of funereal calm. In fact those who do wander in have discovered that museums are now home to many excellent displays interpreting the role of archaeology and its contribution towards an understanding of a locality. Groups of children can often be seen being led, more or less unwillingly, round dimly lit galleries clutching clipboards and worksheets. They are receiving an early introduction to archaeology. The more commercial side of museum life can now be enjoyed as part of the Heritage Industry where attractions such as the 'Oxford Experience' pay a passing acknowledgement to the part archaeology has played in providing a background for their displays.

Out in the countryside families will make visits to stately homes, ruined castles and abbeys, and picturesque villages. Their guidebooks will tell them what they are looking at and if the site is in the care of either The National Trust, English Heritage, CADW or Historic Scotland then there may well be many specific references to archaeological discoveries. In wild areas the dedicated walker may well stumble across archaeology, while navigating across lonely moorland.

By far the most immediate experience most people will have of archaeology is when coming across an excavation. An old row of shops is torn down to make way for development; the hoardings are erected and all of a sudden through the little metal grilles that give a view of the site, people can be seen on their hands and knees scraping away at the ground. In time a sign may go up, bulletins be posted and tours organized for the viewing public. Archaeologists are at work. Everyone enjoys watching other people at work and with archaeology there is a special fascination. Who are these people? What are they doing down there? Have they found anything yet? Seen at a distance there are more questions than answers and frustration can replace fascination as the watcher walks away.

The purpose of this book is to describe what archaeologists do, with the specific aim of inviting the reader to become an archaeologist too. Here is the heart of the matter, for while few individuals have the opportunity to make a real contribution to nuclear physics or space exploration, the opportunities are there for anyone who wants to become involved in making real, lasting and original contributions to archaeology.

Because of the publicity which colours the public's view of archaeology there is still a good deal of misunderstanding of what archaeology can achieve. Archaeology relies heavily on scientific methods. This has not always been the case; many universities still offer archaeology as an arts subject, reflecting its academic origins in classics and divinity, but as archaeology has defined its own area of study and techniques it has become clear that it has become a 'cultural science', like psychology or sociology. This means that archaeologists are part of the scientific community, albeit hovering reluctantly on the fringes sometimes. This idea of community is an important one. It is not restricted to academics or professionals, but those wishing to join must accept scientific discipline. Other archaeologists need to know who you are and how you operate. People who are working as outsiders rarely have their ideas accepted in mainstream archaeology, not necessarily because those ideas are wrong but because they have no standing within the archaeological community.

Scientific disciplines include a respect for evidence, especially in terms of items that can be counted, weighed or measured. In theory, observations should be of the kind that can be checked by an independent observer. In practice, as we will see, some archaeology involves 'unrepeatable experiments' because of the tendency to destroy the evidence as it is examined. Logical thought, making inferences that can be justified by the evidence, and a willingness to test theories in the light of new information are equally valued. There are many other groups who operate around the edge of archaeology. They may subscribe to beliefs relating to the spiritual significance of prehistoric stone monuments and concentrations of psychic energy. This is fine, they may well be right in their beliefs but they will have to study this phenomenon as theologians, not archaeologists.

A good general definition is that archaeology is the study of people in the past through their material remains. The past can stretch back from 'within living memory' (5) to the dawn of the human species. History will often examine the same ground but it depends on written sources and requires a degree of insight and interpretation that qualifies it as an art rather than a science. Related studies are palaeontology which looks at the fossil record of both human and non-human remains and anthropology which looks at patterns of human behaviour. Archaeology can be a great forum for drawing together specialists from other scientific areas. Geologists, biologists, physicists, and chemists have all made contributions to the study of the past, as have photographers, computer engineers, doctors, cooks, crooks, pilots, artists, farmers, musicians and clowns.

15

5 Archaeology does not have to deal with the very distant past. Information on the workings of features such as this lime kiln and the remains of this irrigation system can still be obtained from living informants.

16

The historical background

As well as being about the past, archaeology has its own history. The earliest British archaeologists, in the sense of people who studied the remains of the past for their own sake rather than as part of a quest for treasure, were mainly interested in describing the landscapes around them. A series of great topographers active in the sixteenth and seventeenth centuries travelled the length and breadth of the country recording information about antiquities of all periods. Chief amongst them were John Leland (1503–52), William Campden (1551–1623), John Aubrey (1626–97) and William Stukeley (1687–1765). Their work laid the foundation for landscape studies which continue to this day. Books such as Aubrey's *Monumenta Britannica* are still consulted for the record they provide of monuments in the past, many of which have since been altered or destroyed.

During the eighteenth and nineteenth centuries the landed classes showed much interest in local history and subscribed towards the cost of volumes drawn up to record the history and monuments of individual

6 A page from *The Earthworks of Warwickshire and Worcestershire* by Mr E.A. Downman, a handwritten manuscript from the 1900s.

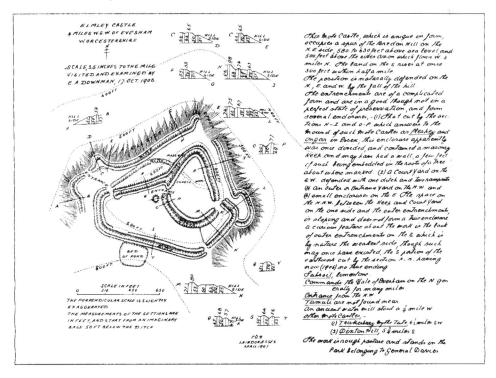

counties (6). Sir William Dugdale's *Antiquities of Warwickshire*, published in 1756, included information on archaeological features as diverse as stone circles and deserted medieval villages. The development of increasingly accurate maps culminating in the founding of the Ordnance Survey in 1791 led to a more precise picture of what was to be found and a number of national societies such as the Society of Antiquaries, founded in 1707, and the British Archaeological Association, which began in 1844, provided a meeting place for those with common interests. County-based groups flourished and dozens were founded around the middle of the last century, including the Dorset Natural History and Archaeological Society (1845), the Wiltshire Archaeological and Natural History Society (1853) and the Cumberland and Westmorland Antiquarian and Archaeological Society (1866).

Their work was largely concerned with collection and classification, a process greatly advanced by the work of Christian Jurgensen Thomsen, a Dane, who arranged the collection of artefacts in the National Museum according to the materials they were made from. From here it was a short step to realizing that there was a chronological link between materials used and period. Hence the familiar terms, Stone Age, Bronze Age and Iron Age that are still used today.

Excavation began in the early nineteenth century as a barely disguised form of grave robbing. Notorious in this connection was Dean Merryweather who over a period of 26 days in 1849 dug up 31 barrows or burial mounds. It has been remarked that this probably represents some kind of world record! A temporary stop was made to this kind of destruction by the work of General Pitt-Rivers. Between 1881 and 1896 the general conducted a remarkable series of excavations on and around the estates he had inherited on Cranborne Chase in Dorset. His work had a breadth of vision with an eye for detail that set a new standard for those wishing to dig (7). Unfortunately only one or two individuals followed his lead and much of what happened in British archaeology in the early years of the twentieth century was little more than trenching along walls to recover the plans of ruined buildings.

More exciting developments were to be found abroad, where individuals such as Sir Austen Henry Layard (1817–94) in the Middle East, Sir Flinders Petrie (1853–1910) in Egypt and Sir Arthur Evans (1851–1941) in Crete made important discoveries about vanished civilizations. They also generated enormous interest and enthusiasm at home which led to fashionable crazes for things antique. Work abroad by these pioneers ensured a steady flow of antiquities back into this country, and set the scene for the development of an academic study of the past at our universities. This was initially founded on a strong tradition of

7　A page from General Pitt-Rivers' 1898 monograph on King John's House. In this investigation he pioneered the technique of combining excavation with the analysis of the fabric of a standing building.

classical studies, but gradually independent departments of archaeology became established.

Meanwhile local societies and museums were digging away in a rather haphazard way with much of the work being very uneven in terms of quality. A particular lack was any sense of development on a site, this was largely a consequence of digging horizontally to recover plans. In the 1930s Sir Mortimer Wheeler (1890–1976) arrived on the scene and in a series of influential digs, as for example at the Roman city of *Verulamium* near St Albans, emphasized the importance of digging vertically. The essence of his method was to lay out a grid across the site and dig in small boxes separated by baulks of earth. The vertical faces of these baulks were drawn in great detail and the sections they produced studied for clues about the chronological sequence of events. He had the natural genius to make the technique work because he was not afraid to break his own rules and open up the site where necessary. Others who followed in his footsteps were not quite as successful. The pendulum had swung too far the other way and the country was peppered with small-scale excavations, working in scatters of tiny boxes. Now the importance of the plan was being neglected and many important clues remained buried between the trenches.

By the beginning of the 1960s archaeology was run by a combination of local and national societies, university departments and museums. On the whole they got on reasonably well together and also with the large numbers of amateurs who provided the labour force for an extensive programme of excavations; excavations which it has to be said were in general large in number and very variable in quality. By far the most common period under investigation was the Roman period, and Roman archaeology was easy in the sense that many of the buildings were of stone so the remains were simple to recognize and dig with a high level of predictability. However, archaeology was poised on the edge of a revolution. As is often the case no single event can be seen as initiating the dramatic changes, rather several things had been happening and suddenly all came together.

Firstly, in the years after the Second World War archaeologists began to take a wider view of their subject and what it could achieve. For example Professor V. Gordon Childe (1892–1957), who had seen developments in prehistory as resulting from a process of diffusion from the Near East, went on to describe two great turning points: the change from hunting and gathering to settled farming communities; and the creation of the first urban settlements. These wider perspectives were given a theoretical framework in the later 1960s by workers such as Lewis Binford in America and David Clarke in Great Britain. Their 'new archaeology' laid stress on the importance of collecting quantifiable data which was then manipulated with a variety of mathematical and statistical tools.

Out in the field 'dirt' archaeologists were developing their own new approaches. Widening interest in prehistoric and medieval sites exposed the weaknesses of the 'digging in a box' system. The more ephemeral of timber buildings were just not making sense viewed through the old 'keyhole' techniques. A number of pioneering excavators such as Brian Hope-Taylor working at Yeavering in the late 1950s and Philip Rahtz digging at Cheddar from 1960 to 1962 demonstrated how large sites can only be understood by a process of total excavation. Baulks were stripped away and large areas exposed so that the full plans of large structures could be seen at once. Complex urban sites proved equally challenging and the work of Martin Biddle at Winchester through the 1960s provided an arena where methods were continually reviewed and refined. Another site that saw this process of continuing technical development was the deserted medieval village at Wharram Percy. Excavation began here in 1950 when Maurice Beresford started trenching for walls. The limitations of this method were soon realized, and by 1953 open area excavations were planned using expertise acquired

8 George Street, Winchester, a small parish church excavated in the late 1950s and laid out for display.

in Denmark. As years went by the scope of the project was broadened to take in the entire history of the settlement and its setting within the landscape.

Through the 1960s there had been something of a development boom, Britain was finally back on its feet after the Second World War and there was a new mood for change (8). Coupled with this were new technologies applied to buildings, roads and farming and suddenly the whole of the nation's heritage was under threat. The hearts of Britain's historic towns were being torn out as foundations were dug for vast shopping centres, broad ribbons of concrete criss-crossed the countryside as new motorways were built and farmers ploughed up old pasture at a fast and alarming rate. RESCUE, a pressure group with the aim of awakening public opinion to these dangers, was founded in 1971. Over the next three years it became hugely successful in persuading the government to raise its spending on archaeology from £210,000 to £460,000 by 1973. It also spawned a large number of locally-based rescue groups, some of which are still operating. Even so, the existing framework within which archaeology had been working seemed unable to cope in this crisis and a new series of regional organizations were set up to deal with the threat.

These new units as they were called were formed by responsible bodies such as local authorities or museums, or independent trusts drawing on government funds. Some were based on existing projects centred on historic towns such as Winchester, Exeter and Lincoln, but

21

the real money went to larger units based on the regions. The first of these was the Oxfordshire unit which opened in the summer of 1973. Southampton and London emerged later that year. Over the next couple of years others followed and were soon busy digging round the clock to gather precious information from the jaws of the bulldozers. These were very exciting times. Financially, though, archaeology was on a shaky footing. The fixing of government grants to units for 1980–81 at the same levels as the previous year in the face of 20% inflation led to redundancies after a period of almost unchecked expansion. It was hardly surprising that archaeologists were keen to make use of the funding opportunities presented by the new schemes set up by the Manpower Services Commission in the early 1980s, intended to relieve unemployment (9).

The scheme had its attractions; more archaeology was being done as new projects were set up and as there was a clear requirement that projects should ultimately be of some benefit to the community, standards of presentation and interpretation were high. There were other side effects which were not so beneficial. Firstly the MSC schemes confirmed a trend which had been growing since the early days of the units, that excavating was something that was done for a wage by full-time diggers. Volunteers were actively discouraged from many sites. A further problem came about when the time came to publish for although money was available to keep large groups of people busy digging, the thought of employing two or three highly-skilled professionals for a year to see the thing through to publication was less attractive. Finally the whole edifice collapsed in 1988 when funding was withdrawn.

9   Lifting the remains of a stained-glass window during excavations of St Stephen's Chapel, Redditch funded by the MSC.

22

Fortunately all was not lost, for in 1986 a voluntary code had been drawn up between the British Archaeological Trust and the Developers Liaison Group. Brian Hobley of the Museum of London was a key figure in securing an agreement whereby in return for time and money the developers expected the archaeologists to work to a timetable and not 'publicly campaign for the preservation of remains *in situ*'. The government supported this code on the basis that 'the polluter should pay' and so we have a system today where most archaeology is developer-funded. Each county authority will pay for its own county archaeologist who runs a Sites and Monuments Record and liaises with the planners. If new proposals seem to pose a threat to archaeology then outside contractors, the old units in a new guise, have to be brought in to assess the site. If important discoveries are made the site has to be excavated at the developer's expense. Of course, as soon as the rate of development slackens then the amount of developer funding is reduced and archaeologists are out of work.

Although the emphasis of archaeology, and particularly the way it is paid for, has changed, the same variety of activities goes on. University departments still teach, local societies still meet, groups organize fieldwalking and excavation and individuals ponder where archaeology will go next.

What do archaeologists do?

Although the perceived threat to the nation's past is not as great as during the rescue boom of the 1970s there is still an enormous amount to be done and not enough people on the ground to do it. It follows that anyone with a real interest and a desire to help will be able to find a part to play. There are plenty of openings and the route taken depends on what sort of archaeologist you want to be.

The work of professional archaeologists will vary in its emphasis depending on the sector they are employed in and their personal interests and skills. Whether working for a national or local authority, a museum, university or unit, certain of the following tasks will take up a portion of their day.

Administration
Because of the complex nature of the work, the variety of sources that funding comes from and the need for extensive consultations, most archaeologists spend what they feel is a disproportionate amount of time filling in forms, writing letters and, worst of all, attending meetings. (10)

23

Fieldwork

Excavation is not the only, nor even the most common, thing that archaeologists do out of doors. As will be seen there are plenty of ways to study the past that do not involve digging large holes. Many archaeologists spend a lot of time recording known sites as they appear on the ground and searching for new ones.

Excavation

Although some archaeologists do contrive to dig throughout the best part of the year, most will restrict their digging to a short season. This is partly to do with the weather but also means that there is time left to process the huge amount of data most digs produce. Even on an excavation not everyone spends their time on their knees with a trowel. Again there are a whole range of specialized activities for those interested.

Research

Both fieldwork and excavation are features of archaeological research, but once the raw data has been collected it has to be studied and some sense made of it all. This could involve extensive reading, attending seminars and conferences and visiting other sites and museums. There are plenty of non-digging archaeologists who make it their business to collect together other people's discoveries so as to produce the definitive guide to a certain type of find or monument or a new theory which pulls together a whole series of observations.

10 Working in the site hut. For every hour spent digging archaeologists will need to spend three or four hours in the 'office'.

Conservation

Once objects are dug out of the ground they start to corrode or decay. Archaeologists, if they are not to be labelled vandals, have a responsibility to preserve those objects and make them available for future study. Some people develop a national reputation for dealing with particular materials, while others develop a range of skills which could be described as 'first-aid for finds'.

Teaching/lecturing

While those working for a university department would automatically expect to take on a major teaching commitment, most archaeologists recognize a responsibility to inform both the public and colleagues about the scope of their work. Many museums and units have education officers working for them specifically to liaise with schools and colleges. (11)

Publication

Most archaeological projects culminate in a publication of some sort, whether it is a slim typed interim note of a season's work or a multi-volume final report. Most of these are the product of a good deal of team work, while someone is drafting the main text others will be drawing plans, preparing photographs or writing specialist reports.

11 Reconstruction plays an important part in education and public relations. This is the reconstructed corner of a defended Iron Age settlement near Guiting Power in Gloucestershire.

25

Career openings in archaeology

While qualifications are not essential for a career in archaeology they certainly help. Most professionals move into archaeology after a first degree, although not always in archaeology. There are historians, fine arts specialists, computer engineers and botanists all working as paid archaeologists. First jobs could include being a full-time finds assistant on a major dig, working for a county council on compiling a record of sites and monuments in the area, becoming a technician in a university department with responsibility for geophysical prospecting equipment, employment with a large unit as site photographer or talking to school children as education officer in a museum, or numerous other possibilities.

There is a strong expectation that most professional archaeologists will want to further their careers by going on to do higher degrees. Some students go straight on to do post-graduate work researching into some topic in order to gain a Ph.D. Having secured a doctorate and perhaps some wider experience they might be taken on to lecture and do further research with a university department. Alternatively they could move into any of the other sectors at higher levels of responsibility perhaps directing excavations, working as county archaeologists or heading departments in large units.

What sort of people get involved in archaeology? Few people would claim to be totally uninterested in our past and many will read books and magazines and watch programmes on the television. Taking the interest further demands something more. It is interesting to note how many top archaeologists were involved in the subject from an early age. The young Mortimer Wheeler was convinced there was a Roman villa at the bottom of his garden and there was! Barry Cunliffe was supervising excavations for Winchester museum at 17 after doing his first fieldwork aged 10. He went on to become the youngest Professor of Archaeology, appointed to a chair at Southampton at 26. John Collis, who is now Professor of Archaeology at Sheffield, dug with him at the age of 12.

Equally there have been individuals who have come to archaeology late in life, perhaps after retirement and have used their time to good effect like Eric Higgs, a Shropshire farmer, who became a respected authority on early European prehistory in his sixties. If there were any characteristics which were common to all the great figures in archaeology they would almost certainly include a profound curiosity about the lives of people in the past and an almost limitless capacity for hard work in sometimes difficult conditions.

Finding out about archaeology

For the newcomer to archaeology there are a variety of options
available. Firstly you can, with the aid of this book and others, go off
and work independently. You can develop your own skills through
reading, visits to museums and fieldwork. As long as you cause no
damage and eventually communicate with someone you will be making
a contribution. A more productive approach is to work with others,
either by joining an archaeological society or by taking part in an
excavation. If you enjoy listening to other people talk about archaeology
you may want to attend lectures or join an evening class. Some of these
have a strong practical element and may lead to a recognized award
of a certificate or diploma. If you are able to take advantage of the
opportunities higher education has to offer then you may want to sign
up for a first degree or a post-graduate qualification with an aim to
making a living out of the subject. About twenty universities offer first
degrees in archaeology either by itself or with some other subject, such
as ancient history or geology. The courses vary widely and the only
way to get an up-to-date guide is to write to individual universities for
a prospectus. A few colleges offer courses either to 'A' level or HND
standard but the picture is changing rapidly.

Societies are organized nationally, regionally, locally and in special
interest groups. The **Council for British Archaeology** is a good starting
point. Although not a society open to individual members it does
represent the interests of archaeology as a whole and has an active
programme of lobbying, research, training and publication. They
produce *British Archaeological News*, essential reading for those who
want to keep up with events and find details of forthcoming courses,
conferences and excavations. There are 14 regional groups who work
with local authorities and who publish regional newsletters which
summarize current work in the area. The **Council for Independent
Archaeologists** is a comparatively new group set up to co-ordinate the
work of both individuals and local societies whilst the **Institute of
Field Archaeologists** is a body for professionals. The most respected
archaeological group is the **Society of Antiquaries** founded in 1707,
membership is by ballot only. The **Young Archaeologists Club** has a
number of local branches and organizes trips for young enthusiasts to
help with fieldwork. The main societies by period are the **Prehistoric
Society**, the **Society for the Promotion of Roman Studies**, the **Society
for Medieval Archaeology** and the **Society for Post-Medieval Archaeology**. All of these bodies are open to general membership and all publish
important annual journals. Special interest groups are far too numerous

to list here but they vary from the Society of Archery Antiquities to the Tiles and Architectural Ceramics Society.

Many counties have their own society and some, such as the Sussex Archaeology Society, run their own museums and own a variety of historic properties. Most will also publish transactions where information on local sites is written up. Their commitment to field-work and excavation will vary, depending largely on who is currently involved and what their interests are. The same is true of the smaller groups, based on a town or even a single village. These are even more influenced by the composition of their membership. The local library will be able to give you information about relevant groups. A well-run society is there to serve the needs of its members and should be responsive to any new initiatives that people wish to propose. Of course, if all else fails you can always start your own group!

Another important source of information, and encouragement, will be the curatorial staff at local or county museums. If these individuals are not archaeologists they will certainly have a keen interest and some knowledge of the local area and will be used to fielding casual enquiries of the type 'My daughter dug this up in the garden, what is it?' A serious archaeological enquiry would best be made to the county archaeologist's department, which the 'front of house' staff will be able to put you in touch with. The odds are that your county archaeology service will be working under considerable pressure and may not welcome casual callers. However, an appointment arranged either by letter or telephone will do much to smooth the way. The key tool for answering most local enquiries is the county **Sites and Monuments Record** (SMR). This is basically a list which draws together all that is currently known about the archaeology of an area and should contain information about everything from major ancient monuments to chance finds made during building work or ploughing. The record is usually available for interested parties to examine and the staff responsible for its upkeep will always welcome new information to add to it.

One of the best ways to keep in touch with what is going on is to subscribe to any relevant journals. The best of these is *Current Archaeology*, established in 1967. It has recently been improved with a new larger format and colour illustrations. The editors, Andrew and Wendy Selkirk, have strong opinions on the role of the amateur or 'independent' archaeologist; coverage is detailed and well presented. *Minerva* is an attractive periodical but it does tend to concentrate on finds more than sites perhaps because the publishers, B.A. Seaby, are coin and antiquities dealers. The Council for British Archaeology print their *British Archaeological News* six times a year for subscribers,

28

while if you are a member of English Heritage you will receive their own magazine every two months. If you live within the London area *The London Archaeologist* is essential reading. The national newspapers can be very unpredictable in the amount of space they give to archaeological stories. It is generally recognized that the *Independent* has the edge at the moment.

The archaeologist and the law

The legislation that surrounds planning and development as they relate to monuments, conservation areas and listed buildings is quite complex. As far as the fieldworker is concerned, however, the principles are simple but it is essential to find out about them.

All land and any items found on that land are owned either by public bodies or private individuals. Permission must be obtained by anyone wishing to work on someone else's land, especially if they expect to be taking away finds.

Most recognizable sites are protected as scheduled ancient monuments. This means that it is an offence to damage them in any way or remove any materials from the site. The message is look but do not touch!

Many old buildings are listed by the Department of the Environment and English Heritage, CADW and Historic Scotland as being of special historical interest. This places important restrictions on what can and cannot be done to such a property but basically no alterations can be made without permission of the local authority.

All of this of course harmonizes with the archaeologist's wish to study the past without adding to the considerable amount of destruction that is already going on. It also underlines the fact that excavation cannot even be contemplated without the widest possible consultation both locally and nationally.

2 Getting out and about – basic fieldwork

Reading the landscape

The British landscape has evolved over the centuries, creating a pattern that is full of meaning to the trained observer. We can only understand our present environment by reference to the past. Although archaeology does not offer any easy answers to our planet's present predicament an understanding of where we have been must shed some light on where we are going. The important thing about our surroundings is that while each generation has made its additions to the landscape they have not wholly removed traces of earlier occupation, at least not until the twentieth century.

I was once working on a local history project based on a large post-war housing estate. The social history of the community was fascinating

12 Neithrop, Banbury, the 'forty-million-year-old' hedge.

and the houses were interesting as early examples of pre-fabrication in concrete; but the biggest puzzle was an old hedge. It had many mature trees along its line and was clearly much older than the surrounding homes. Study of maps from the last century helped us to realize that the hedge was a lone survivor of the pattern of fields that had been laid out across the hillside in the eighteenth century. However, the question persisted, why here? We looked more closely at our maps and discovered that the hedge was following the line of an earlier track from the town out towards a hamlet on top of the hill. It had followed the line of a shallow valley to ease the climb. The hamlet had all but disappeared by the sixteenth century and the track had become disused. But still the question, 'why?' Why was the valley on this particular part of the hillside? Finally we turned to a map of the local geology which showed a series of fault lines running across the face of the hill. This weakness had led to the formation of the valley which had dictated the position of the track which had influenced the placing of the hedge. The hedge which was now home to waste paper and empty drinks cans had a pedigree which stretched back some forty million years (12)! That demands some respect so we did the very least we could do: we cleared away the litter!

Making visits to sites and monuments

A good way to begin to develop an interest in archaeological sites is by making a programme of visits to well-known monuments where there is already a certain amount of information available. Sites and monuments open to the public fall into the care of a number of bodies. English Heritage (with sister organizations CADW for Wales and Historic Scotland) is responsible for most of the major prehistoric, Roman and medieval sites in Britain. Membership qualifies you for free entry to sites and the *Guide to English Heritage Properties*. This tells you where sites are and more importantly when they are open (13). The National Trust owns wide tracts of land which include a number of monuments; other sites are owned by local authorities or are in private hands. The best guide to these are the twin publications *Museums and Galleries in Great Britain and Ireland* and *Historic Houses, Castles and Gardens Open to the Public*. The former of these has entries on sites ranging from La Hougue Bie, a Neolithic tomb from around 3000 BC on Jersey to the nineteenth-century Biggar Gasworks Museum in Lothian.

Many thousands of people visit these sites each year and yet the

13 Two faces of English Heritage: (*Above*) A medieval Fair in progress at Kenilworth Castle. (*Below*) Keep off! The excavated remains of Wolvesley Palace, Winchester.

suspicion sometimes begins to form that many people are missing out on much of what the site has to offer. This is not to suggest that it is not very pleasant sometimes just to enjoy a site for its scenic beauties or to indulge in a little nostalgia, but the beginnings of real understanding will only come through a certain amount of critical examination.

It is always worthwhile to try and do some reading before visiting a site, guidebooks to English Heritage sites can be purchased from their postal sales department or from the HMSO. These give some idea of what to watch out for or particular points to study; also, the relevant Ordnance Survey maps can give a feel for the monument in its setting. Once at a site read the guidebook thoroughly through once, perhaps underlining items of special interest. For many years English Heritage and its predecessors sold detailed and authoritative pamphlets. These days, however, there is a move towards highly-illustrated guidebooks which are strong on visual appeal but can be weak on detail. This echoes a common trend over the past few years towards increasing amounts of interpretation and less hard evidence. Again this is fine providing you bear in mind that you are being given one person's particular view of the site; your agenda may be different, so plan your own visit. You can tour a site chronologically, searching out the earliest remains first. Industrial sites are perhaps best viewed by following the routes that processed materials would have taken. Some sites can be explored according to their function: for example, you might like to begin a castle tour at an outer gatehouse and penetrate the layers of defence until you reach the keep.

It is important to take time to stop and look rather than just walking round immersed in a guidebook. A powerful aid to observation is sketching. Even if you are no artist it is still worth taking a sketch-book along to record details that interest you (14). An additional yet related activity is to attempt your own reconstruction drawings. This is a valuable exercise which can be applied to most archaeological sites. Even at a fairly basic level it will make you confront some of the key issues about how a monument functioned in the hands of its original occupants. As an alternative to sketching taking good quality photographs with a 35 mm single lens reflex camera mounted on a tripod will help you in exploring the site in order to find the best angles to take the most informative pictures.

As you explore make critical use of the guidebook. Although it is unlikely there will be many obvious errors, try to pick out those points which are speculative and make notes of your own ideas. Also make notes of points of interest that are not covered by the guide; this must necessarily carry only a very abridged account of the site. It is common

33

14 (*Left*) Cogges Manor Farm Museum, Oxfordshire, sketching details of a medieval window.

15 (*Right*) Portchester Castle, Hampshire. Beyond the medieval wall lies the Roman fort, an outer earthwork and the harbour they were built to defend.

practice to tour a monument from the inside only but try not to let your horizons be closed in by the surrounding walls. Try to develop an understanding of why the site is where it is. If a vantage point is available, climb it and then with the map in hand assess the surrounding area. If the work is defensive why was this site chosen (15), if industrial how were materials carried to and from the location?

Landowners of properties adjacent to tourist attractions can be rather sensitive about trespassing but wherever possible tour the area around to view the site from the outside. Most monuments are associated with a host of other landscape features, many of them of great interest in their own right and generally neglected by the majority of visitors. Kenilworth Castle in Warwickshire is a good example of this (16). There is certainly plenty to see, but those who explore the buildings and then turn around and return to their cars are missing much: massive earthworks, a priory, the site of a pleasure garden and the castle fish ponds!

34

Museum visits can also be more productive if approached in the right way. Most people at some time experience museum fatigue as they wander past the umpteenth display and wonder where the tea-shop is. Some planning can avoid this. When arriving at a large museum it is certainly a good idea to have a quick look round to get one's bearings and a feel for the style of presentation the museum favours. By this time you should have some specific items in mind that you will want to return to for study. Again a sketch-pad is a useful adjunct for making notes and drawings, but remember that most museums only have a fraction of their collection on view at any time. If you do have some special interest it is essential that you contact the curatorial staff in advance and they will be able to tell you what arrangements can be made to view the reserve collections.

Exploring off the beaten track

The outings described so far are all to some extent 'packaged'. The kind of experience you have is determined by the way the site is organized. At some venues visitors are actually strapped into cars and

16 Visiting Kenilworth Castle.

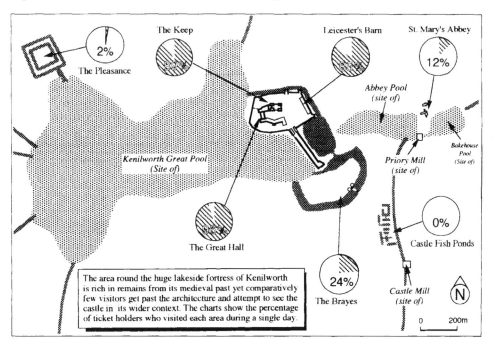

<table>
<tr><td colspan="3">The area round the huge lakeside fortress of Kenilworth is rich in remains from its medieval past yet comparatively few visitors get past the architecture and attempt to see the castle in its wider context. The charts show the percentage of ticket holders who visited each area during a single day.</td></tr>
</table>

trundled round at a pace designed to get the optimum number of people round in any one day. Individuals who want to broaden their understanding sooner or later will have to strike out on their own and do a little genuine exploring. There are many ways to begin. You could get to know one or two rural parishes or a small town, or you might want to examine a particular kind of site that has captured your interest, water-mills or hillforts for example.

Finding sites

Maps are the primary source of information on what to see and where it can be found. The Ordnance Survey's 'Landranger' and 'Pathfinder' maps both mark monuments of all periods in a medieval style typeface, except for Roman sites which are shown in classical looking capitals. In addition the larger scale Pathfinder maps will show the layout of monuments above a certain size. Of course these maps only show a proportion of the known sites and only in very general terms. For detailed coverage on a county by county basis you will need to turn to the Sites and Monuments Record mentioned earlier. These are set up in such a way that they should be able to answer all queries about a particular locality or type of monument. Volumes such as the *Victoria County Histories* published by the University of London and the inventories of the *Royal Commission for Historic Monuments* give a general guide, but there is still the possibility of finding new and unrecognized sites. We shall return to these important sources of information later on.

This book does not attempt to tell the story of Great Britain as it has been revealed by the work of archaeologists; but to make sense of some of what follows it is necessary to look at the main periods in British history, and how they are represented in terms of field monuments.

Period	Dates (approx.)	Sites or Monuments					
		Religion	*Burial*	*Settlement*	*Defence*	*Industry*	*Agriculture*
Neolithic	4500 BC to 2500 BC	Henge, Cursus	Long barrow	Causewayed camp	?	Axe factory	?
Bronze Age	2500 BC to 700 BC	Stone circle	Round barrow	?	?	*Metalworking site*	Reave

Period	Dates (approx.)	Sites or Monuments					
		Religion	*Burial*	*Settlement*	*Defence*	*Industry*	*Agriculture*
Iron Age	700 BC to AD 43	*Temple*	Barrow, *Cemetery*	Farm	Hillfort	*Metalworking site*	Celtic field
Roman	43 to 400	*Temple*	Barrow, *Cemetery*	*Villa*, Town	Fort, Town wall	*Kiln*, Quarry	Celtic field
Early Medieval	400 to 1100	Cross, Church, Abbey	*Cemetery*	*Village*, Town	Burgh, Motte and bailey	*Kiln*, Quarry	Lynchet Ridge and furrow
Medieval	1100 to 1500	Cross, Church, Abbey	Graveyard	Village, Town	Castle, Moat	*Kiln*, Quarry	Lynchet Ridge and furrow
Post-Medieval	1500 to Present Day	Church, Chapel	Graveyard	Village, Town, City	Artillery Fort	Furnace, Factory, Mill	Enclosed field

Items in *italic* are not normally seen as field monuments. Any particular class of monument is not necessarily in use for the whole period indicated.

Glossary

Barrow – A mound which marks a burial place, sometimes called a tumulus.

Burgh – A defended town, usually surrounded by an earth bank.

Causewayed camp – An enclosure surrounded by concentric yet broken rings of bank and ditch

'Celtic field' – Small rectangular fields, normally surviving as earthworks.

Cursus – A 'processional way' defined by low parallel banks.

Enclosed fields – Fields laid out in the post-medieval period when the strip fields were gathered together to make larger units. Often rectangular, surrounded by hedges.

Henge – A circular, ditched enclosure with an outer bank.

Lynchet – Terracing on a hill side to facilitate cultivation.

Moat – An enclosure, usually rectangular, surrounded by a ditch that was water-filled.

Motte and bailey – An early castle, based on a large mound, or motte, with a defended courtyard or bailey, attached.

Reave – A low stone bank which surrounds early fields.

Ridge and furrow – Low parallel banks: ridges mark the sites of thin strip-like fields, separated by shallow hollows or furrows.

It seems extraordinary on such crowded little islands as Great Britain that anything fresh could turn up, but things do and in some cases whole classes of monuments gain new recognition. In 1972 Andrew Fleming and John Collis rediscovered and re-interpreted a vast system of prehistoric land boundaries or reaves, on Dartmoor. Another example is to be found in the remains of gardens. For many years these were misinterpreted or ignored, but it is now appreciated that their earthwork remains are a common and important feature of the rural landscape. I was once leading a course on fieldwork on Exmoor when my group stumbled across a hitherto un-noted alignment of standing stones in Culbone Wood. Our delight turned to chagrin when the county archaeologist informed us they had been reported to him by another fieldworker just a week earlier!

Once more maps are an important tool for these kinds of discoveries. Large-scale maps can be examined for unusual features that may be clues to the existence of new sites. Many L-shaped ponds have turned out to be remains of medieval homestead moats. Parish boundaries sometimes follow disused roads, tracks or other earthworks, while strangely-shaped fields or patches of woodland may follow the outline of unknown defensive enclosures.

Many sites are in rural surroundings and if you are to move confidently around the countryside you will need to make use of some of the 120,000 miles of public footpaths. All land, no matter how derelict it appears, belongs to someone and much of it is used for periods of intense activity by the farming community. Trespass, although not a crime, can lead to civil suits for damages. The real risk, however, is of antagonizing the landowners on whose goodwill much archaeology depends. If you want to explore, stick initially to public rights of way which enable you to travel safely across private land. This idea of travelling is an important one for it is the key to what you can and cannot do on a public footpath. A footpath is a highway and its only purpose is to enable you to complete a journey from place to place. You can legitimately remove or circumvent any barriers across a footpath which hinder that journey, but that is all. Should a landowner or an agent try to bar your way you may firmly but politely continue, although prudence would advise turning back. Although nobody would normally object to you taking photographs or even stopping to sketch on a footpath circumstances could arise where you could be charged with causing an obstruction.

Many of the upland sites in southern Britain sit in broad swathes of open pasture some distance from any habitation, so you can feel reasonably relaxed about stepping off the path. The thing to remember is that if you are approached you have no alternative but to apologize and leave; you are in the wrong. If a site is fairly close to a working farm it is both courteous and sensible to ask permission to enter the land. This is not to say that it does not require a certain amount of nerve to walk up the drive to a strange front door, perhaps accompanied by a chorus of noisy dogs. However, over the course of the past quarter of a century I have knocked on hundreds of such doors and only been turned away on one or two occasions.

Exploring areas of moorland, mountainside or forest is slightly easier and there are many places where it is possible to move a little more freely. There sometimes exist agreements between landowners and local authorities to permit access, while elsewhere a right of public entry may have been established by custom and usage. Landowners such as the National Trust and Forestry Commission open some of their many acres to walkers. Areas of special appeal have been designated National Parks. This does not give automatic rights of access to all parts, but you are more likely to find a comprehensive network of well-marked paths.

All users of the countryside should know and observe the country code. If you are going well off the beaten track you will need to consider questions of appropriate clothing, footwear, emergency supplies and first-aid. In addition you should always tell someone where you are going. There have been instances of archaeological groups working on areas of high moorland getting into difficulties, so make sure you are well aware of the hazards and can cope with them before tackling wilderness walks.

The British Isles are fortunate in being covered by some of the best large-scale maps in the world. The Ordnance Survey has done much to advance the progress of archaeology. For initial survey work there are the two essential sets of maps, already mentioned. Firstly, the 1:50,000 maps known as the 'Landranger Series of Great Britain'. The 204 maps provide coverage of the whole country, each one depicting an area of 1600 sq. km (approx. 600 sq. miles). They give a good overview of an area, facilitate getting around the countryside by road and are useful in planning walks in outline. However, for detailed study the 'Pathfinder Series' at a scale of 1:25,000 are vital. These sheets normally cover an area of 200 sq. km (approximately 70 sq. miles), although some in tourist areas are larger. Because of the detail they show, especially footpaths as they relate to the boundaries of individual fields, they are indispensable. In addition they are at a large enough scale to show the plans of many earthwork features. This can be especially useful when trying to get your bearings on the ramparts of a large hillfort. For work on a small area even larger scale maps can be bought. It does pay dividends to take time to become familiar with the conventions on these maps and to practise relating them to the surrounding countryside. One of the main features of Ordnance Survey maps is the National Grid. This is a system whereby any location in the country can be precisely referred to by a combination of letters and numbers called the grid reference. Instructions on how to determine a grid reference are written into the explanatory keys printed with each map.

When out searching for archaeological sites you will need to master some very basic navigational skills. This is partly to help you get about but also, if you do make an original discovery, you will need the means to describe its location. To help with this you will need a magnetic compass of the 'Silva' type. By using the map and compass together you will be able to orient or 'set' the map so that it lines up with the surrounding landscape. Instructions with the compass will show how to take bearings in a number of situations to help with navigation. The next section will look at ways in which the compass can also be used to help draw up plans.

17 Hillfort plans from Volume II, Part 3 of the Royal Commission on Historical Monuments' Inventory for Dorset. (Reproduced by permission of the Royal Commission on the Historical Monuments of England.)

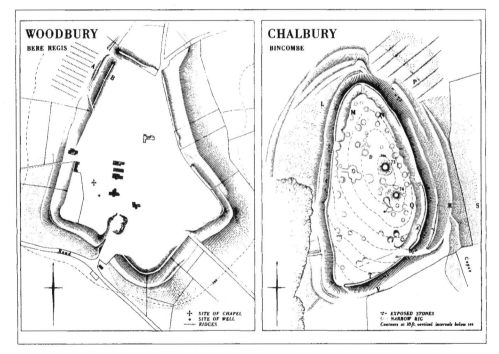

40

Published plans of sites can be very variable in quality. Most counties have an introductory volume in the *Victoria County History* series which will probably contain some fairly rudimentary earthwork plans. On the other hand counties such as Dorset and Northamptonshire which have been studied by the Royal Commission on Historical Monuments will have volumes full of accounts and plans which are both elegant and accurate (17). None of this means that you should not make your own record of a well-known site. Not only is this good practice, but also no monument remains unchanged. An up-to-date plan, especially if it highlights recent alterations, can be very valuable. Some county Sites and Monuments Records are short of detailed plan coverage and someone may be able to give you a list of places where some degree of checking up would be welcome.

Starting on surveying

Just as a field guide is necessary when collecting mushrooms or watching birds so there is a need to illustrate the main categories of site you are likely to come across in exploring the historic landscape (20–22). Unfortunately no two monuments are alike so the best that can be done is to select a site that is fairly representative of its type. Most of the remains encountered in lowland Britain will be earthworks: banks and ditches, mounds and hollows. In upland areas where stone is more widely available, cairns replace mounds and banks of rock, ramparts. (18)

Much of the earlier tradition of fieldwork did indeed see archaeological sites like some rare kind of bird that had arrived in the landscape as if they had just happened to land there. Any site only begins to make sense if viewed as part of the total landscape. This involves both its overall setting and the links that exist on the ground with other sites. These include recognizable sites such as castles or burial mounds, but later you will have to show as much interest in springs and streams and ponds, in hedgerows and ancient woodland and in paths, trackways and roads.

In order to represent a three-dimensional earthwork on flat paper a number of conventions are used. For instance, slopes are shown by lines called hachures; their precise size and shape are related to the profile, position and gradient of the slope (19).

When it comes to making your own plans there are several methods available which demand varying amounts of time and equipment. The technique looked at in this section produces fairly accurate sketch plans very quickly. However, it is far from being precise and serves only to

18 Not all monuments are 'earthworks'. (*Above*) Cairn and stone circle near Kilmarin, Strathclyde, Scotland. (*Below*) Burial chambers, Llanenddwyn, Gwynedd.

give a general layout of a site and indicates the scope for further investigation. It makes use of a magnetic compass of the 'Silva' pattern, a metre ruler and your own body.

The compass is necessary to record the bearings along which you walk as you survey the site (**23**). This is easily done: holding the

19 (*Above*) Hachures, conventions for drawing slopes. (*Below*) Measuring a slope.

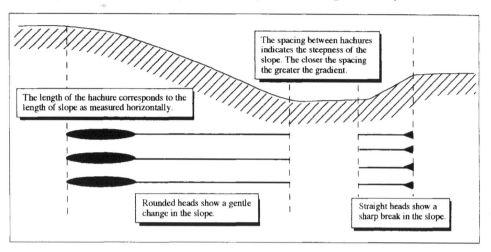

The spacing between hachures indicates the steepness of the slope. The closer the spacing the greater the gradient.

The length of the hachure corresponds to the length of slope as measured horizontally.

Rounded heads show a gentle change in the slope.

Straight heads show a sharp break in the slope.

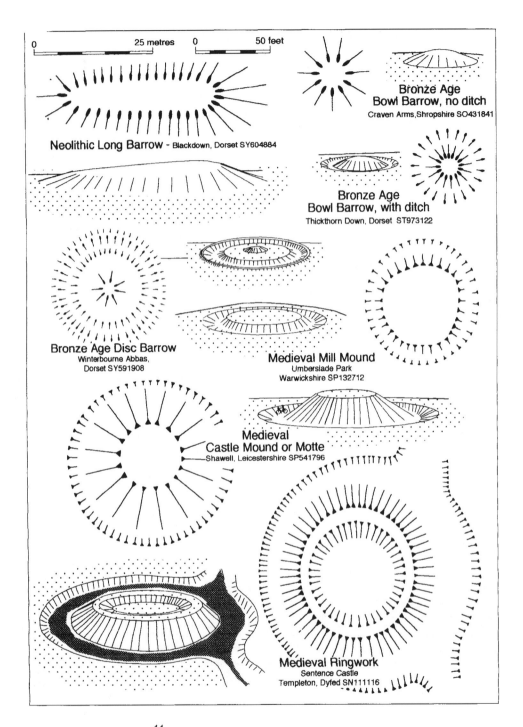

0   25 metres   0   50 feet

Neolithic Long Barrow - Blackdown, Dorset SY604884

**Bronze Age
Bowl Barrow, no ditch**
Craven Arms, Shropshire SO431841

**Bronze Age
Bowl Barrow, with ditch**
Thickthorn Down, Dorset ST973122

Bronze Age Disc Barrow
Winterbourne Abbas,
Dorset SY591908

Medieval Mill Mound
Umberslade Park
Warwickshire SP132712

**Medieval
Castle Mound or Motte**
Shawell, Leicestershire SP541796

Medieval Ringwork
Sentence Castle
Templeton, Dyfed SN111116

44

compass flat on your hand, point the arrow on the outside of the case in the direction of travel. Turn the dial until North is opposite the red end of the compass needle. Read the bearing off against the original arrow. You will also need to know what your average walking pace is. To do this measure in metres the distance you travel in walking a hundred paces and divide this by a hundred. Make a note of this figure: it will be both useful and surprisingly accurate. Leslie Grinsell, a bank clerk who became the recognized authority on Bronze Age burial mounds, visited almost 20,000 of them and measured the majority by pacing.

The first crucial task before beginning to survey is to have a good look round to make sure you have an idea of the limits of the site. For the purposes of this exercise imagine you are drawing a plan of a motte-and-bailey castle. Having toured the site, begin by drawing out roughly the line of the perimeter of the bailey, round the top of the bank. Slopes are shown approximately using short lines. Choose a starting point and face along the top of the slope. The next step is to divide up the curving bank into a series of straight lines. This can either be done in the mind's eye or by actually setting markers into the ground. Take a bearing along the first of these sections and then pace the distance until forced to turn. Record a new bearing and pace on until once more it is necessary to stop and take a new line. This continues all the way round the top of the bank. These lines can be drawn out roughly and the bearings and paces written next to them.

Later on these measurements will be redrawn to give an outline from which to work, but also required are the height and width of the banks and ditches and the large mound. The vertical height and the length of the slope are recorded as measured against its face. This will have to be done at several points round the perimeter to record the changing profile of the defences. Once more use a non-standard but known measure: your height from ground- to eye-level. First make a free-hand drawing of the profile of the banks and ditches you have chosen to measure. Do not forget to mark on the plan where these sections are. Standing in the bottom of the ditch look directly at the bank keeping your eyes level and fix a place to go and stand on. Climb up the bank to that point, stand up and look again. This second point you fix on is now twice your height above the ditch and so you proceed, climbing the slope and measuring it in multiples of your own height. With some practice this can be accurate to the nearest metre on large banks. The heights of smaller slopes can be estimated using a metre stick as a guide. On the way back down the metre stick is used to measure the length of the slope as well as the width of the bottom of any ditches and the top of any banks (24).

20 (*Opposite*) Mounds: plans and views of some typical examples.
21 (*Overleaf*) Enclosures: plans and views of some typical examples.
22 (*Overleaf*) Large enclosures: plans and views of some typical examples.

45

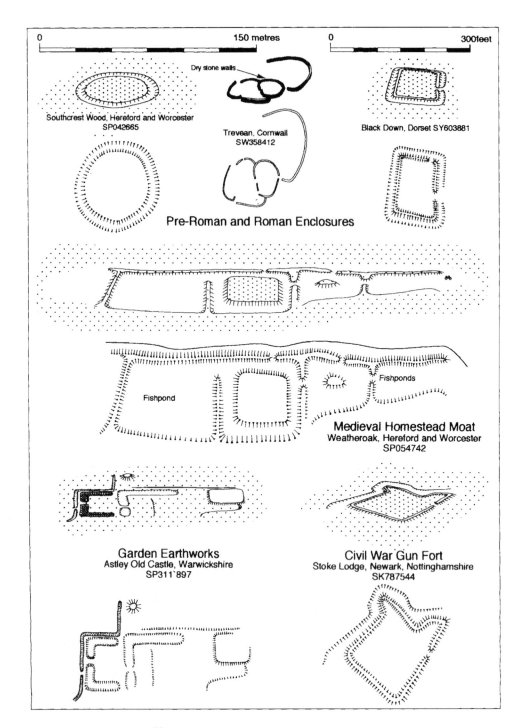

0   150 metres   0   300feet

Dry stone walls

Southcrest Wood, Hereford and Worcester
SP042665

Trevean, Cornwall
SW358412

Black Down, Dorset SY603881

Pre-Roman and Roman Enclosures

Fishpond

Fishponds

Medieval Homestead Moat
Weatheroak, Hereford and Worcester
SP054742

Garden Earthworks
Astley Old Castle, Warwickshire
SP311`897

Civil War Gun Fort
Stoke Lodge, Newark, Nottinghamshire
SK787544

46

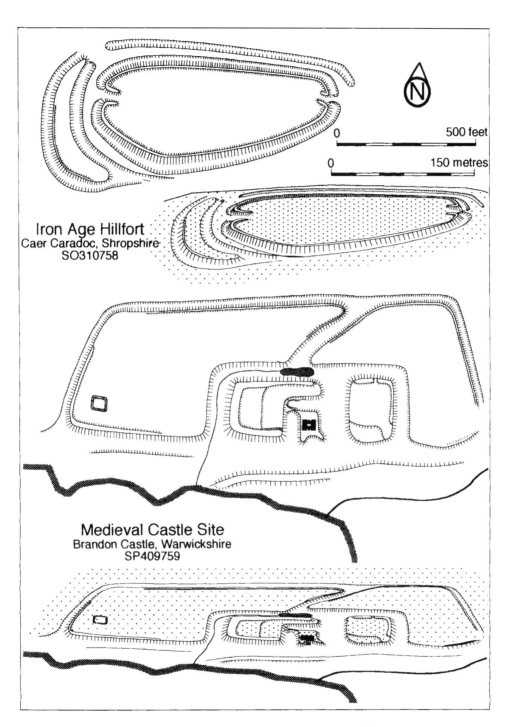

Iron Age Hillfort
Caer Caradoc, Shropshire
SO310758

Medieval Castle Site
Brandon Castle, Warwickshire
SP409759

0   500 feet

0   150 metres

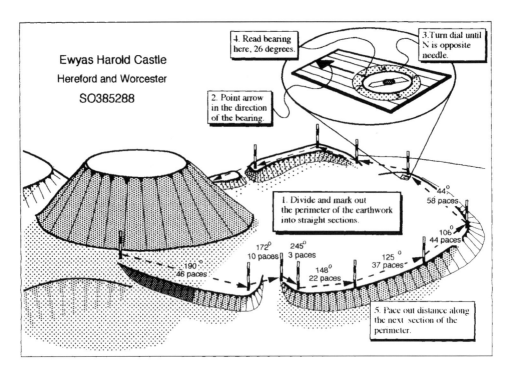

Ewyas Harold Castle
Hereford and Worcester
SO385288

4. Read bearing here, 26 degrees.

3. Turn dial until N is opposite needle.

2. Point arrow in the direction of the bearing.

1. Divide and mark out the perimeter of the earthwork into straight sections.

44°
58 paces

106°
44 paces

172°
10 paces

245°
3 paces

125°
37 paces

148°
22 paces

190°
46 paces

5. Pace out distance along the next section of the perimeter.

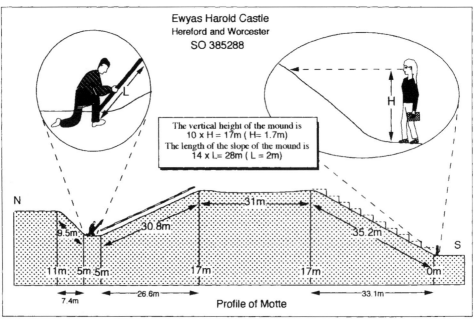

Ewyas Harold Castle
Hereford and Worcester
SO 385288

The vertical height of the mound is
10 x H = 17m (H= 1.7m)
The length of the slope of the mound is
14 x L= 28m (L = 2m)

L

H

N

9.5m

30.8m

31m

35.2m

S

11m 5m 5m   17m   17m   0m

7.4m

26.6m

33.1m

Profile of Motte

48

Back at base you can begin to convert your rough notes and drawings into a finished sketch plan (25). The first thing to do is to convert all of the non-standard measurements into metres. Then decide on a scale. As the castle is roughly 200 metres (approx. 650 ft) square, a scale of 1:1000 will give an image which will fit on to a sheet of A4 paper. A larger scale of say 1:500 might be more appropriate for recording greater detail on an image that would be 40 centimetres (16 in) square.

Having decided which way is North, a bearing of 0/360 degrees, use a protractor and a ruler to begin to plot the bailey's outline. This is drawn as an irregular polygon which will then have its corners rounded to produce a more natural effect. The next step will be to make scale drawings of the profiles of the mound and banks and ditches. By combining the height and length of slope it is possible to measure the horizontal width of the slope as we will need to draw it on to the plan.

Knowing the widths of the bank tops and ditch bottoms will help in drawing a series of concentric rings round the outline which mark the tops and bottoms of the different slopes. Finally a new set of marks can be added: the hachures. To complete the plan add on the profile drawings and other essential information: the name of the site and a full grid reference, the date it was surveyed and by whom, the scale and a pointer indicating North.

On sites such as barrows or small castle mounds a couple of profiles measured at right angles to each other will normally be all that is needed, but on more complex sites additional bearings will be necessary to tie different parts of the site together. On something as intricate as a large deserted medieval village site you may have to be very selective about what you record, aiming to produce a general plan which can be refined if necessary at a later date by a full-scale survey. Plan making is an important aid to observation and you may come to a number of conclusions about the development of the site as you work around it. An attempt can be made to set things in their correct chronological sequence by noting which features cut across other features and are therefore later, and which features are partially buried by others and so are earlier (26).

Any record you keep will include other information you have collected. You might want to draw your own location map (27) to pick out relevant features in the landscape and record points the Ordnance Survey map may have neglected or not be up to date on. As part of your written notes you will probably include details about how the land is being used, what damage or threats there are to the site, something about its general state of preservation and any relevant information you may have picked up, such as local names for the site,

23 (*Opposite, above*) Using compass bearings to plot the outline of an earthwork.
24 (*Opposite, below*) Measuring the profiles of slopes.
25 (*Overleaf*) Stages in drawing a plan based on compass bearings.
26 (*Overleaf*) A complex earthwork site and its interpretation.

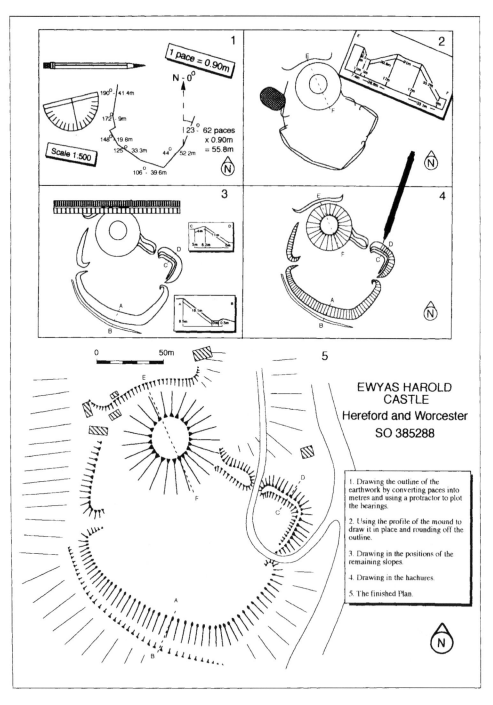

1. Drawing the outline of the earthwork by converting paces into metres and using a protractor to plot the bearings.

2. Using the profile of the mound to draw it in place and rounding off the outline.

3. Drawing in the positions of the remaining slopes.

4. Drawing in the hachures.

5. The finished Plan.

EWYAS HAROLD
CASTLE
Hereford and Worcester
SO 385288

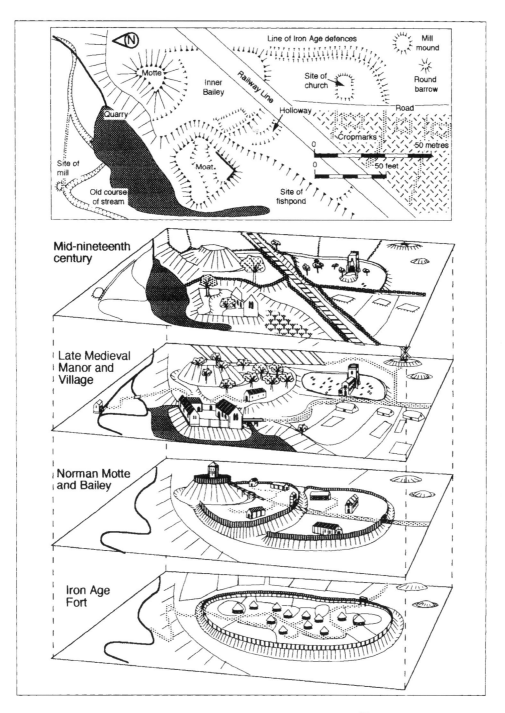

Mid-nineteenth century

Late Medieval Manor and Village

Norman Motte and Bailey

Iron Age Fort

Legend (top panel):

N

Motte

Inner Bailey

Railway Line

Line of Iron Age defences

Mill mound

Site of church

Round barrow

Quarry

Holloway

Road

Site of mill

Moat

Cropmarks

Old course of stream

Site of fishpond

0 ___ 50 metres

0 ___ 50 feet

27 A simple location map.

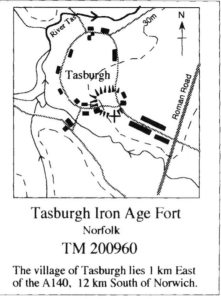

Tasburgh Iron Age Fort
Norfolk
TM 200960

The village of Tasburgh lies 1 km East of the A140, 12 km South of Norwich.

28 (*Opposite, above*) Celtic fields near Worth Maltravers in Dorset. An informative picture of a difficult subject which succeeds because of appropriate choices of viewpoint, time and equipment.
29 (*Opposite, below*) Using raking light to bring out surface details. Ridge and furrow, medieval fields at Arlescote, Warwickshire.

or finds that have been made in the area.

The area where you are working may have ploughed fields around. Although ploughing reduces and eventually removes earthwork remains it can also expose buried materials such as scatters of building debris or patches of dark soil along the line of former ditches or hollows. These features can be planned and recorded and notes made about the kinds of materials which are visible. There will also be more specific finds. Flint tools, fragments of pottery and small pieces of metalwork all turn up frequently in the plough soil. They are, of course, important additional clues about the past of any particular area and should not be removed in a haphazard way. In the next chapter we will look closely at fieldwalking and the structured collection of such evidence. This is not treasure hunting.

Much can be done to record a site photographically (28–9), although earthworks are notoriously difficult to photograph well. Most archaeologists working in the field will use a 35 mm single lens reflex camera for speed and convenience. The best combination is of a wide angle lens, say 28 mm for general site photographs and some close-up work, together with something like a 70–150 mm telephoto zoom lens for picking out sites from a distance. It is useful to include a scale in any pictures you take to give some idea of size (30). At a pinch a person

52

30 Using scales. Bank barrow and adjacent round barrows, Broadmayne, Dorset.

will do, but a properly painted photographic scale looks more business like. Strong wooden dowelling, 2 m long and painted alternately black and white at 50 cm intervals, will do for photographing most sites and if it is strong enough it can double as a measuring rod.

Although you may view much of this as part of a personal training programme or just an activity to give added interest to a Sunday afternoon walk you should not undervalue the exercise. You may stumble across something new and even on well-known sites a watching brief backed up by documentation can become an invaluable record of a site's unfolding history. By compiling a folder of plans, photographs and notes you will not only be developing your own expertise but also be creating an archive that could be very valuable in the future.

Working with buildings

So far we have been dealing with sites where the only surviving remnants are humps and bumps on the ground, but increasingly archaeologists have turned their attention to intact buildings. A standing building survey is an activity well suited to the beginner. It is interesting, immediate and is the kind of job that really needs doing. Whether work is being done on a parish church, a derelict factory or a small country cottage the procedures are the same. A particular need at the moment is for the recording of vernacular architecture, in other words the common-place buildings of the town and country (31). These were erected by local builders working as part of a local tradition. As well as houses, examples include farm buildings and small industrial premises. While pretty country cottages are at risk from no more than the efforts of the home improver, many associated outbuildings are being demolished wholesale.

Obviously there are very few buildings that you can just walk into and start work on. It is vital to obtain the necessary permissions and more importantly secure the trust and confidence of the owner or occupier. This is where membership of a local society can be necessary; this will help establish a context for your studies which will dignify them in the public eye as something more than simple curiosity. Most home owners are fascinated by the history of their own house. Providing you are prepared to make initial contact by letter, conduct some preparatory interviews and make appointments to work at convenient times you will mostly be made welcome. The trade off for the disturbance caused, as far as the occupier is concerned, should be a full report and set of plans and elevations of their property.

As with earthworks the starting point for any investigation of the material remains is a series of scale drawings. However, this time the third dimension becomes much more significant. With a standing building you will find yourself not only drawing plans of each floor but also side views or elevations of each of the walls. Because much of a building's history is expressed in its details you may well find yourself

31 Small-scale nineteenth-century 'industrial' buildings, Cropredy, Oxfordshire. On the right a small barn used by the village stone mason, on the left a cobbler's workshop from the 1900s. The path joining the two is made from fragments of gravestones.

55

making a stone-by-stone drawing of a wall or sketching details of a joint on a smoke-blackened roof timber. Taking measurements of a building is easier than working with banks and ditches which rarely have definite starting and finishing points. A wall is reassuringly solid when it comes to measurement but it also calls for greater precision. You will certainly have to invest in at least one large tape measure, a 30 m one is ideal. A retractable 2 m metal hand-tape, or a 2 m folding-rule will also prove useful.

The plans of most buildings will be based on a series of rectangles. This simplifies recording as long as you remember that the shapes are unlikely to be regular, you will need to measure the two diagonals as well as round all four sides. The convention for buildings is to draw the plan of features as if the structure had been sliced through at window height so all openings will be shown. Further complications arise with old buildings in that the walls themselves may not be straight and their thickness may vary (32).

For an initial survey some of these difficulties may have to be ignored. Work ought to begin with a general tour to establish the character of the building and its overall layout. A sketch plan of the ground floor can then be made and annotated with those measurements necessary to fix the proportions of the rooms, establish the size and position of features such as doors, windows and fireplaces and determine the thickness of the walls at various points. Other period details such as partitions or sinks should also be included. More elaborate surveys could take in details of old floor boarding or ceiling joists. Further notes will probably need to be added to your plan as a record of the materials used and as a reminder of features which you may want to come back to to photograph or draw in more detail. This whole procedure may be repeated on the first floor and in the attic. A scale of 1:20 is probably best for this work although complex arrangements of fixtures and fittings might be better drawn at 1:10 and larger groupings, for example round a farmyard, might need to be done at 1:50 or even 1:100.

The walls of many old buildings are a patchwork of blocked up windows and doorways, different materials and methods of construction and scars where structures have been removed (33). The correct recording and assessment of these clues will reveal the building's history. Drawing elevations not only captures the character of the building as it stands but also facilitates this kind of interpretation. Detailed stone-by-stone drawing is a sophisticated business which demands some technical resources, most notably scaffolding. However, there are easier alternatives. If the wall has been plastered or rendered, or is fairly

32 Cottages in Cropredy, Oxfordshire showing the buildings illustrated above. The larger of the two cottages was built around 1580 while the smaller was added in the mid-eighteenth century.

56

GROUND FLOOR PLAN

Store

Store

Scullery

Proposed Dining Room

A

up

Living Room

Workshop

Bathroom

Kitchen

FIRST FLOOR PLAN

SECOND FLOOR PLAN

Bedroom 2

Bedroom 3

Attic Room 2

up

Landing

Landing

Attic

Bedroom 1

Attic Room 1

featureless then you should be able to draw an elevation by eye and put on certain crucial measurements as an aid to drawing it out accurately. Again for most small buildings a scale of 1:20 is most useful although 1:50 may be better for simple elevations of larger buildings.

Any activity which takes the feet off the ground ought to be thought through carefully. In a domestic setting some measurements can be made from the windows of upper floors with the aid of a long tape measure. You may choose to work from a ladder against an outside wall but this can be risky. Certainly any ladder you intend to use should be secured in place, top and bottom. An inventive answer to this problem as an alternative to a ladder is the use of a home-made lightweight set of aluminium rods, marked at 10 cm intervals, which can be slotted together to measure heights up to 10 m.

You may be faced with situations, perhaps where the structure is either extremely tall or ruined and dangerous, of having to make assessments of height from a distance. An approximate measure can be made by stepping well back and using the width of your thumb at the end of an outstretched arm to move up the feature being measured. This will give you a height expressed in multiples of your thumb which can be converted into a more useful form by 'measuring' the width of your thumb against a feature you can then get close to at a similar distance and measuring that.

33 Brimstage Hall, Cheshire. A pattern of blocked windows and scarred walls reveals a complex story of building and rebuilding.

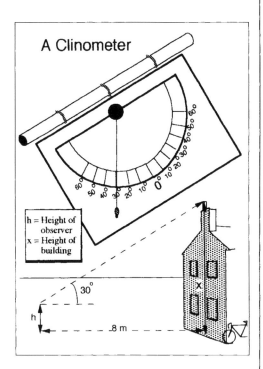

34 Using a clinometer.

If the sun is shining you can measure the length of the building's shadow. By relating that to the length of shadow of an object of known height you can calculate the unknown figure this way:

$$\frac{\text{Height of building's shadow}}{\text{Height of known object's shadow}} \times \text{Height of known object} = \text{Building's height}$$

If the sun refuses to shine then you will have to use a **clinometer**. Although these are available commercially, and are part of the built-in functions of a theodolite, a simple version can be made at home. It consists of a board, the top of which is used to sight along. Drawn out on the side of the board is a protractor to measure the angle at which an attached plumb bob is hanging. As you lift the clinometer to peer at the top of the feature you are measuring, the string of the plumb bob will move to register the angle you are looking up at. This information needs to be recorded as does the distance you are standing away from the base of your feature (34). These measurements can be converted into a scale drawing which will give you a fairly accurate height. Alternatively, if you are prepared to work a fixed distance away

59

from the features you are measuring then the clinometer can be directly calibrated with the heights observed.

If more detail is needed on your wall elevation you can turn to photography. This will not only provide a good visual record but can in some circumstances be used to produce a scale drawing. Photogrammetry, as this technique is called, in the hands of experts demands expensive equipment and a high level of expertise to achieve extraordinarily precise results. At a more basic level much can be done with a 35 mm camera, a 50 mm lens to minimize distortion, and a step ladder. You will also need a slide film and a scale. The process involves standing as far back as possible from the wall in a position as near as you can to the middle of the wall. This is where the step ladder comes in. Now take your photograph making sure your scale appears on it.

Once the slides have been developed you can project them on to drawing paper. If you have decided to work at a scale of say 1:10 then you will draw a line 20 cm long on the paper. By adjusting the distance between the projector and the paper you can enlarge or reduce the image until the 2 metre scale on the picture matches the 20 cm line on the paper. Now you can start tracing the details on to the paper. This

35 The development of a terrace of cottages in Cropredy, Oxfordshire.

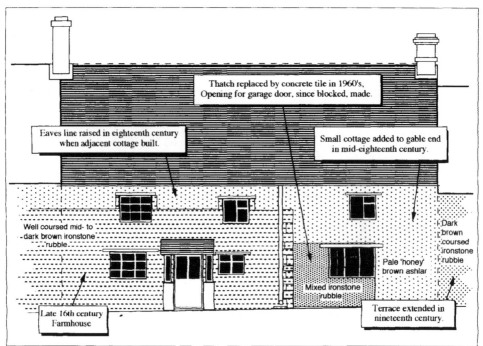

Thatch replaced by concrete tile in 1960's, Opening for garage door, since blocked, made.

Eaves line raised in eighteenth century when adjacent cottage built.

Small cottage added to gable end in mid-eighteenth century.

Well coursed mid- to dark brown ironstone rubble.

Dark brown coursed ironstone rubble

Pale 'honey' brown ashlar

Mixed ironstone rubble

Late 16th century Farmhouse

Terrace extended in nineteenth century.

method works well with walls up to around 5 m tall. You will need to fill as much of the frame as possible so you will normally be able to capture about 6 or 7 m of wall in this way. Of course longer stretches will have to be covered by a series of overlapping pictures.

You will almost certainly have to record timber structures (37) as part of a building survey, either as part of the whole house if it is timber framed or else in the roof. A combination of photographs, sketches and perhaps scale drawings will all be needed to make a comprehensive record (35–6). As with all recording of this kind your aim should be to record in sufficient detail so that even if you do not understand the full significance of everything you are looking at someone else looking at your material will. Hundreds of historic houses are being demolished every year and many more are being remodelled inside to the point where historic features will be lost or covered over. Again, your record could become of great significance.

As with earthwork remains, your understanding of any particular building will be enhanced by examining and recording something of its setting (38). For a house this means exploring the surrounding village or town, with a church, the churchyard, if you were looking at a factory you would also want to investigate workers' housing and transportation.

Later on we will look at questions of publishing information about any projects you have been working on but as a starter you should

36   (*Left*) Drawing an elevation of an eighteenth-century cottage at Byfield, Northamptonshire. Because the cottage is built on a slope a levelled line has been put up to measure from.

37   (*Right*) Structural timbers from the medieval mill at Bordesley.

61

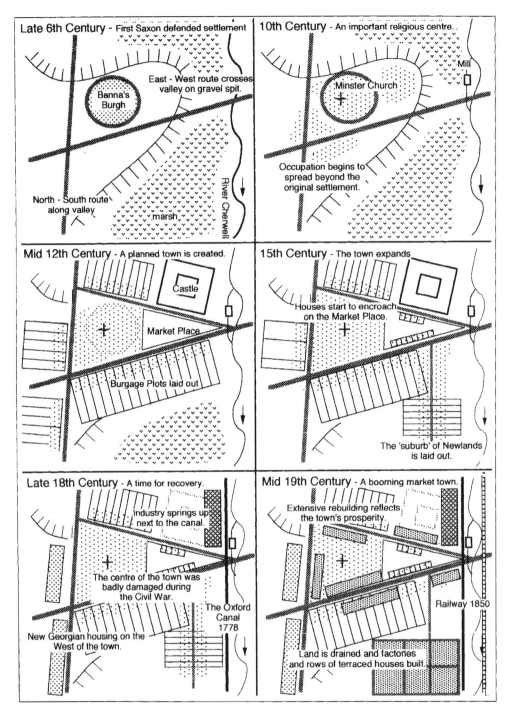

Late 6th Century - First Saxon defended settlement

East - West route crosses valley on gravel spit.

Banna's Burgh

North - South route along valley

marsh

River Cherwell

10th Century - An important religious centre.

Mill

Minster Church

Occupation begins to spread beyond the original settlement.

Mid 12th Century - A planned town is created.

Castle

Market Place

Burgage Plots laid out

15th Century - The town expands

Houses start to encroach on the Market Place.

The 'suburb' of Newlands is laid out.

Late 18th Century - A time for recovery.

Industry springs up next to the canal.

The centre of the town was badly damaged during the Civil War.

New Georgian housing on the West of the town.

The Oxford Canal 1778

Mid 19th Century - A booming market town.

Extensive rebuilding reflects the town's prosperity.

Railway 1850

Land is drained and factories and rows of terraced houses built.

always try to find somewhere to deposit copies of any finished notes or plans you have. As well as the Sites and Monuments Record, local libraries may be happy to take copies. If your work is centred on, for example, a single parish, then a parochial church council may hold a copy in the parish chest. Give or send copies of relevant work to landowners or indeed anyone else interested. The goodwill engendered will more than make up for the cost of photocopying.

38 (*Opposite*) The development of Banbury; it is important to consider individual monuments within their setting.

3 Real research – field survey projects

Many students of archaeology will eventually want to embark on a serious study of some aspect of their surroundings with a view perhaps to publication. This will involve learning new techniques, investing in some additional equipment and almost certainly beginning to work with others. One important focus for research that we will not examine in detail here is the use of old maps and other documents as an aid to understanding archaeological features. The benefits of conducting field-work hand-in-hand with other historical investigations have been demonstrated many times. The normal starting point for documentary research will be the county record office. There are always staff on hand to help but the field is such a huge one that they will only be able to assist with very general enquiries. This is another area that the aspiring fieldworker has to become familiar with.

Advanced survey methods

The approaches to site planning looked at in the previous chapter were quick and convenient. However, what they gain in simplicity they lose in accuracy. These 'snap-shot' surveys are fine in an emergency or where a very quick overview of several sites is required but a long term investigation working towards publication can afford to be a little more sophisticated. The following three survey methods do not demand huge quantities of equipment but do take time and attention. As the plan will normally be drawn on site it is easy to cross check against what is on the ground and if necessary repeat measurements to ensure accuracy. Teams of three are ideal for this work, one to draw the plan and two to handle the measuring equipment.

To begin with you will need at least two 30 m tape measures for each group surveying. Although not cheap they are a vital part of any survey work. They should never be put away wet or muddy, used in tug of war contests or dragged unnecessarily along the ground. A large ball of string and some tent pegs can be used to mark out base lines where necessary and a collection of ranging rods, the kind of red and white poles surveyors use, are helpful for marking out the site. Suitably painted garden canes can be used as a much cheaper but less durable alternative. As an additional aid each pole can be labelled with a card flag carrying a letter by which it can be referred to.

A large portable drawing board and a selection of drawing implements complete the kit (39). Generally people prefer to draw with a hard pencil, 4 or 6H and will then use a technical drawing pen with waterproof black ink for finished work. Some people are happy to make simple scale conversions in their heads and use an ordinary ruler, but for difficult scales and increased confidence a scale ruler can be bought. These usually have a variety of graduations set to certain scales so that 14 m at a scale of 1:500 can be measured directly producing a line 28 mm long. For triangulation you will either need a conventional drawing compass with an extension bar or else a beam compass. On this the point and the pencil can be moved independently along a long rigid

39 Some basic equipment for survey work.

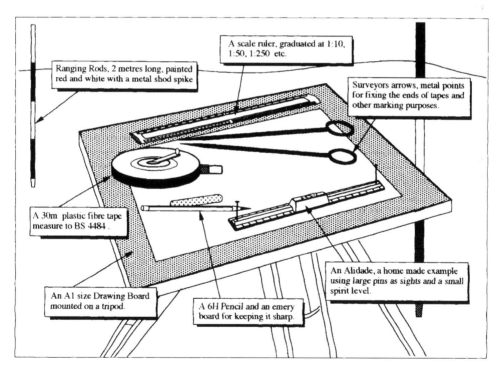

A scale ruler, graduated at 1:10, 1:50, 1:250 etc.

Ranging Rods, 2 metres long, painted red and white with a metal shod spike

Surveyors arrows, metal points for fixing the ends of tapes and other marking purposes.

A 30m plastic fibre tape measure to BS 4484.

An Alidade, a home made example using large pins as sights and a small spirit level.

An A1 size Drawing Board mounted on a tripod.

A 6H Pencil and an emery board for keeping it sharp.

bar. Most archaeologists doing serious survey work will draw on to a plastic film. This can be worked on either in pencil or ink and is tough, dimensionally stable, weatherproof and very expensive. It can be bought from most shops dealing in drawing equipment.

Planning by offsets

The first method involves laying out one or more base lines and then plotting the position of relevant features by measuring along the base line then out at right angles, these are the offsets (40). If you are working with a sheet of gridded paper under your drawing film it is an easy matter to convert the measurements to scale and draw them in. Most people can judge a right angle fairly accurately by eye; however, there are a number of techniques which can improve on this. The easiest is swinging the tape. The shortest distance from the point being measured to the base line has to be at a right angle so the correct figure is guaranteed by pulling the tape taut and swinging it from side to side until the shortest measurement is found. The base line and tapes will only be able to reach an area 60 m wide so on large sites there will be a need to establish further baselines to ensure the whole area is covered. A right angle can be set out on the ground by measuring a 3,4,5 triangle. Some people have employed a Roman surveying instrument called a *groma* to help in setting out. This has a square board on which are set two sights at right angles. By lining this up with the base line an offset can be positioned accurately by peering along the second sight.

Triangulation

The great advantage of this method is that it can easily be made self-checking so that any errors show up and can be corrected. Once more it begins with a base line which is marked out and measured to scale on to the plan. A tape is then positioned at each end of the base line and measurements taken from each to the feature which is to be marked on the plan. On the drawing board these two measurements are converted to scale and then drawn as arcs with a compass (41). The spot at which the two arcs intersect gives the planned location of the feature. Pin-point accuracy can be ensured by incorporating a third tape working from a different place on the base line. If all three arcs now intersect you can be confident your positioning is precise.

As before, larger sites will have to be covered with a network of triangulated points which may be far from the original base line (42). In these circumstances it is particularly important to mark with ranging rods key points that are being worked from.

40 Surveying by offsets, a variety of techniques.

Badgworthy Deserted Medieval Village
Devon
SS 793445

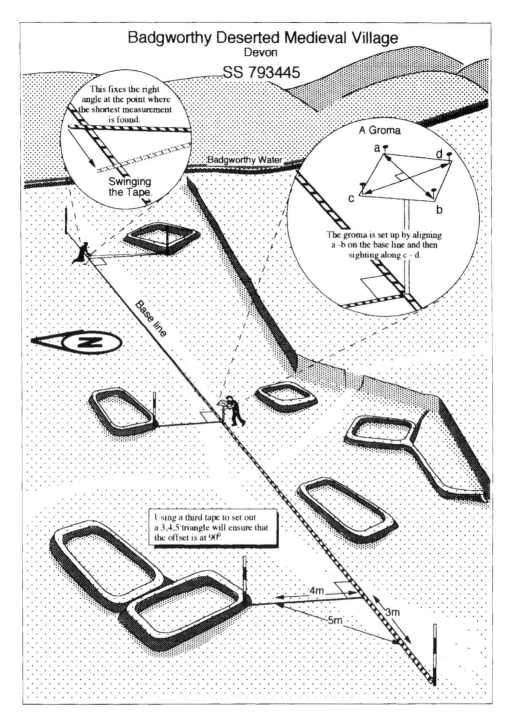

This fixes the right angle at the point where the shortest measurement is found.

Swinging the Tape.

Badgworthy Water

A Groma

a

d

c

b

The groma is set up by aligning a - b on the base line and then sighting along c - d.

Base line

N

Using a third tape to set out a 3,4,5 triangle will ensure that the offset is at 90°.

4m

3m

5m

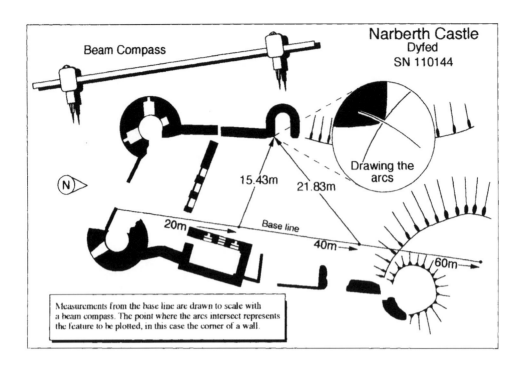

Beam Compass

Narberth Castle
Dyfed
SN 110144

Drawing the arcs

15.43m

21.83m

20m

Base line

40m →

60m →

Measurements from the base line are drawn to scale with a beam compass. The point where the arcs intersect represents the feature to be plotted, in this case the corner of a wall.

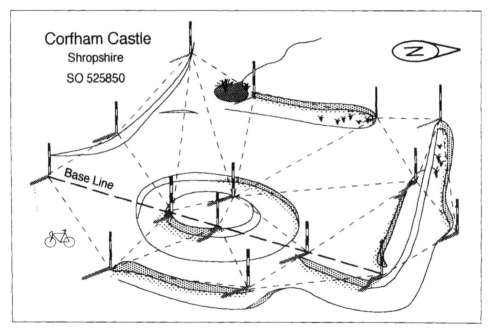

Corfham Castle
Shropshire
SO 525850

Base Line

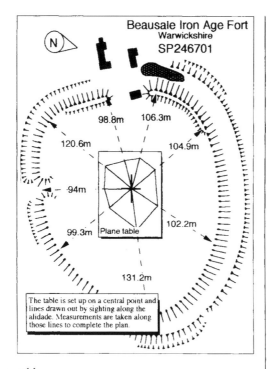

Beausale Iron Age Fort
Warwickshire
SP246701

98.8m 106.3m

120.6m 104.9m

94m

99.3m Plane table

102.2m

131.2m

The table is set up on a central point and lines drawn out by sighting along the alidade. Measurements are taken along those lines to complete the plan.

43 Planning by radiation.

Working with a plane table

Plane tabling can be less labour intensive than the first two methods but does require some additional equipment. The first of these is the plane table itself, a drawing board mounted on a tripod with the facility to set it up so that the board is exactly level. Also needed is an *alidade*, this is simply a ruler with a sight attached. Home made versions of both pieces of equipment can be constructed fairly easily. On site there are two main methods to use, these are radiation and intersection.

To plan by radiation the table is set up in a commanding position near the centre of the site (43). Marking your position on your plan you can then use the alidade to draw out radiating lines to the points you want to record. As these may be some way away it is as well to mark them with ranging rods to sight on to. The distance from the table to the rod can then be measured on the ground and drawn on to the plan.

The second method involves a base line once more and is a variety of triangulation but workable over greater distances. The table is set up at one end of the base line and its position marked on to the plan. The alidade is then used to sight on to crucial points and lines drawn to show in which direction they lie. The table is then moved to the other end of the base line and the new position marked. The procedure is repeated from this new spot, sighting on to the same points. The

41 (*Opposite, above*) Fixing a point by triangulation.
42 (*Opposite, below*) Covering a large site by triangulation.

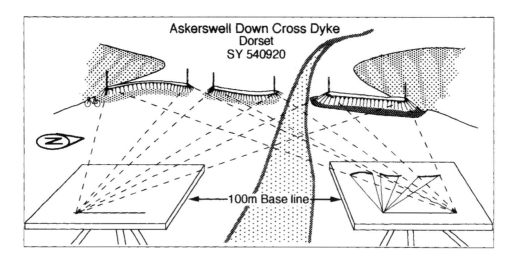

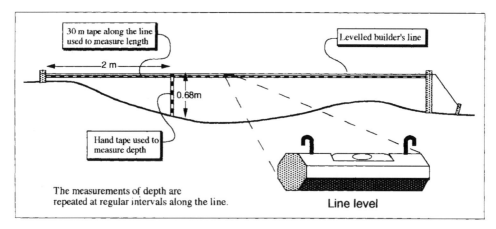

44 (*Above*) Surveying by intersection.
45 (*Below*) Using a line level to draw an earthwork profile.

lines you draw will intersect fixing the position of the relevant points on the plan (**44**). This technique can be used to accommodate points which cannot easily be reached.

Levelling

As we saw in the last chapter, drawing the outlines of features is only part of the job, attention also has to be paid to questions of height and depth. On a typical earthwork site it will be necessary to measure the profiles of the banks and ditches so their limits can be faithfully recorded on the plan. A method which is fairly straightforward to use on low banks and shallow ditches involves setting up a line and measuring down to the ground surface from it. A builder's line and a *line level*, a small spirit level with hooks that can be hung on the line, are needed (**45**). To set the line up, it is tied on to a peg driven into the ground at the higher end and on to a wooden stake at the lower end. Its position can be adjusted using the line level at the middle of the line to ensure it is truly level. The line will need to be pulled as tight as possible so it does not sag. A 30 m tape is then stretched out along the line and a hand tape used to measure down to the ground at regular intervals. This can be drawn up on site as a kind of vertical planning by offsets. For very deep ditches or high banks you may have to set up a combination of lines to cover all the ground.

If you can get your hands on one by far the best piece of equipment for this kind of work is an *optical level* (**46**). This is a small telescope set up on a tripod which can be accurately levelled. Once in place the telescope can be turned round to sweep round a level field of view. If a large 'ruler' is now introduced on to the scene it is possible to measure the distance from the optical plane down to the ground surface at any point within sight of the telescope. In practice a large graduated staff, normally made from aluminium and expandable up to 6 or 8 m, is used. The staff is marked in centimetres to make it easily readable even at some distance. The measurements and calculations are recorded in a specially formatted level book which should always be to hand should any rechecking be necessary.

46 Using an optical level to draw an earthwork profile.

71

47 A contour survey.

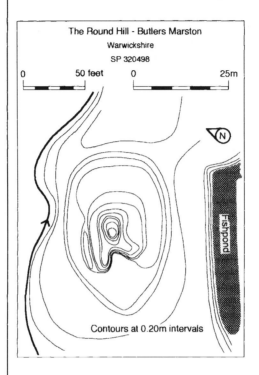

The Round Hill - Butlers Marston
Warwickshire
SP 320498

0   50 feet   0   25m

N

Fishpond

Contours at 0.20m intervals

A line can be set up as before and the depth of the ground below the level measured at regular intervals. An optical level can also be used for contour surveys (47). Some sites benefit from being recorded in this way and a grid is set up across the area under study and spot heights recorded from the level. These are written on to a plan of the grid and the contour lines plotted by eye.

At some stage you will need to tie in your measurements with a standard reference point, called the *site datum* (48) and ultimately with the Ordnance Survey datum: the height above sea level. To do this a spot is chosen, one which you are reasonably confident will remain unchanged and which you can return to repeatedly. If no such point is immediately available some people create their own by sinking a large block of concrete into the ground on a secure foundation. Once this site datum is established all measurements are made with respect to it and are recorded as being so many metres above or below site datum. The usual procedure is to set up the level and take an initial reading on to the site datum. This measurement is carefully recorded in the level book and other readings subtracted from it in order to express them as they relate to site datum. A negative answer of course indicates that the point is below the site datum. The height of the site datum can be determined by levelling across country until you come to a benchmark. The locations of these are shown on the maps and their precise height, if not shown, can be obtained from the Ordnance Survey.

The exact combination of methods you choose for your survey will depend on the nature of the site and the resources you have available. On a large settlement site you might use plane tabling to record the boundaries of the site and offsets to record details of internal structures. A levelled line could be used to record profiles of a surrounding bank and ditch while the optical level is employed for a contour survey of the interior. As long as care is taken to relate the different elements of the survey to each other everything should be fine.

There are a number of key principles which underlie all survey work:

a Always walk round the whole site and prepare a sketch plan first. This will help you decide how to tackle the work.
b Always work from the whole to the part. This means planning the broad outlines first and then filling in the detail.
c Always make whatever independent checks you can on your measurements. Do not become blinded by science or confused by detail, step back every now and then and compare your drawing with the real thing. They should match up.

48 Determining levels from a site datum.

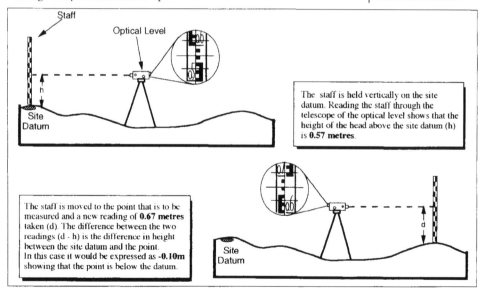

The staff is held vertically on the site datum. Reading the staff through the telescope of the optical level shows that the height of the head above the site datum (h) is **0.57 metres**.

The staff is moved to the point that is to be measured and a new reading of **0.67 metres** taken (d). The difference between the two readings (d - h) is the difference in height between the site datum and the point. In this case it would be expressed as **-0.10m** showing that the point is below the datum.

d Always record on the plan the name of the person drawing it, the date, the scale, the direction of North and the location and name of the site.

e Always work slowly and methodically.

Aerial photography

Some of the most dramatic and revealing views of sites and their setting within the landscape are enjoyed by birds. In the course of any piece of survey work it is always useful to be able to share that view and endless ingenuity and invention have gone into achieving this. The normal features of the landscape will be visible although earthworks are only fully revealed under a slanting light which casts long shadows. Other features, otherwise invisible, will also sometimes figure in aerial photographs. These tend to show up as a result of differences in plant growth which are influenced by conditions in the soil below them (49).

In order to get an aerial view, the most obvious course is to find someone with an aeroplane, climb in with your camera and off you go. This is not quite as easy as it sounds but it can be done. Private pilots have to do a certain number of hours regularly to hold on to

49 The effects of buried features on plant growth.

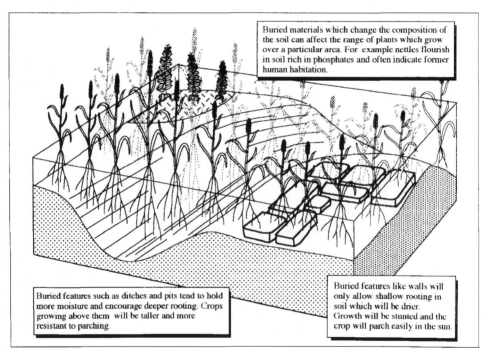

Buried materials which change the composition of the soil can affect the range of plants which grow over a particular area. For example nettles flourish in soil rich in phosphates and often indicate former human habitation.

Buried features such as ditches and pits tend to hold more moisture and encourage deeper rooting. Crops growing above them will be taller and more resistant to parching.

Buried features like walls will only allow shallow rooting in soil which will be drier. Growth will be stunted and the crop will parch easily in the sun.

their licences and will often welcome the chance of a financial subsidy to get them aloft. However, there are problems that need to be addressed. A private pilot cannot take passengers for hire nor can photographs taken be used for commercial gain. Some people take to the air in balloons, microlites and hang gliders, all of which have been used for archaeological work.

If getting yourself into the air is out of the question there are other alternatives being experimented with around the country. These include kites, tethered balloons, radio-controlled aircraft and hydraulic booms. The basic requirements are that the camera can be raised and lowered safely and can be triggered at some distance, again radio control comes in here. More sophisticated systems include a video link with the video camera mounted alongside the stills camera so the shutter can be triggered to secure exactly the right view. I know of groups who have enlisted the help of local engineering companies, college design departments and even the army to good effect. In fact there are many 'aerial' views that can be had from the ground and archaeologists will often make use of adjacent hills or look across from one side of a valley to another to get these kinds of distant prospects.

50 Swerford, Oxfordshire. Patterns of medieval cultivation show up in the foreground while the outlines of a motte-and-bailey castle can be made out behind the church with the sites of fishponds beyond that.

Of course your area may already have had useful aerial photographs taken (50). There are several centres to which enquiries can be directed although the best starting point would again be the county Sites and Monuments Record. The largest collection of aerial photographs is held by the Cambridge Committee for Aerial Photography at the University. Both the National Monuments Record and the Ordnance Survey hold extensive collections which can be viewed by appointment. There are also commercial companies such as Aerofilms Ltd which have useful material available at a price. Other large companies and some local authorities who are engaged in big construction or development projects may have aerial cover they are prepared to share, again it is a question of looking around.

Geophysical prospecting

Over the past forty years a range of techniques have been developed which enable the archaeologist to 'see' features otherwise invisible below the ground (51). Machines of this kind work on one of three basic principles. Resistivity meters measure changes in the ground, primarily due to the amount of water it holds, by passing an electric current through it and measuring the resistance. Magnetometers record disturbances in the earth's magnetic field caused by iron rich deposits, burnt or baked clay and other materials. Ground penetrating radar directs radio waves into the earth and builds up a picture of buried features by analysing the information that bounces back. All three systems work best when the data is processed by computer to eliminate the kind of background 'noise' that creeps in and distorts the picture.

The use of these devices and the interpretation of their results require considerable training and expertise normally found in professional units, museums or university departments. However, some of the larger societies do have access to this kind of equipment and may be able to make it available. In the right hands prospecting of this type can reveal a host of buried features but it will not pick up everything and so negative evidence has to be treated with great caution.

Church surveys

In the last chapter we looked at survey techniques on standing buildings, particularly with examples of vernacular architecture. Many of the same methods can be applied to more ambitious projects, church surveys amongst them. The scale of this kind of work and the intense local interest it can generate makes it well suited to a group approach.

Most churches have their own guidebooks and just about all of them are covered in Pevsner's magnificent *Buildings of England* (and Scotland

51 The results of plotting resistivity and magnetic data; examples from Guiting Power, Gloucestershire.

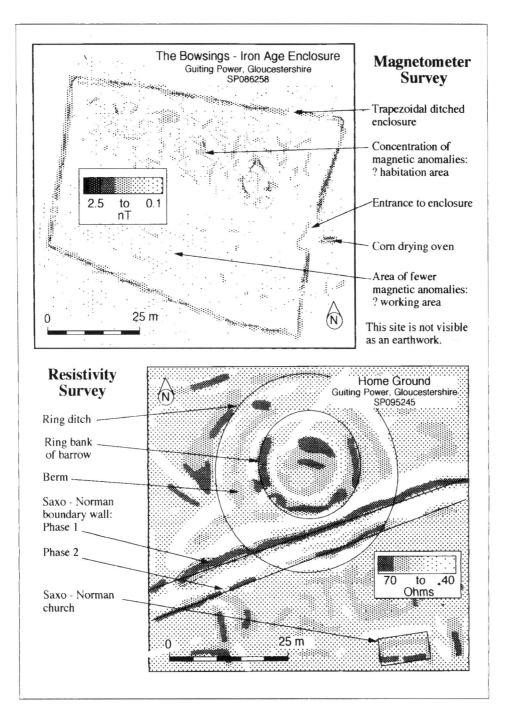

The Bowsings - Iron Age Enclosure
Guiting Power, Gloucestershire
SP086258

Magnetometer Survey

2.5 to 0.1
nT

0 — 25 m

N

Trapezoidal ditched enclosure

Concentration of magnetic anomalies: ? habitation area

Entrance to enclosure

Corn drying oven

Area of fewer magnetic anomalies: ? working area

This site is not visible as an earthwork.

Resistivity Survey

N

Home Ground
Guiting Power, Gloucestershire
SP095245

Ring ditch

Ring bank of barrow

Berm

Saxo - Norman boundary wall: Phase 1

Phase 2

Saxo - Norman church

70 to 40
Ohms

0 — 25 m

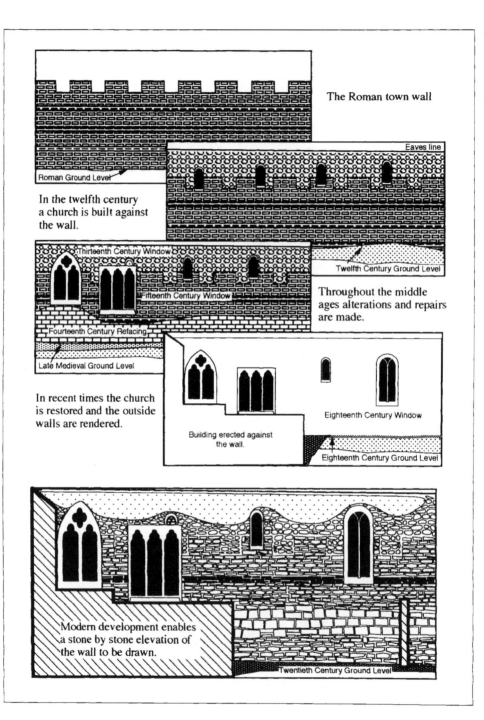

The Roman town wall

Roman Ground Level

In the twelfth century a church is built against the wall.

Eaves line

Twelfth Century Ground Level

Throughout the middle ages alterations and repairs are made.

Thirteenth Century Window

Fifteenth Century Window

Fourteenth Century Refacing

Late Medieval Ground Level

In recent times the church is restored and the outside walls are rendered.

Building erected against the wall.

Eighteenth Century Window

Eighteenth Century Ground Level

Modern development enables a stone by stone elevation of the wall to be drawn.

Twentieth Century Ground Level

78

and Wales) series, published by Penguin. However, a close study of most published materials will show them to have their share of errors. This is either because the church was subject to a rather cursory inspection or because the guide was written with very little reference to the fabric of the building. There are, therefore, ample opportunities to revise and update church guides and in some cases completely reinterpret a building's history.

As before the starting point is an accurate measured survey. Many earlier surveyors ignored the irregularities in line and angle that medieval architecture was subject to. Clues that come from minor changes in both a wall's alignment and its thickness can shed light on how the building has developed. Similarly a stone-by-stone analysis of the way a wall is built and what it is built from can reveal the way in which quite fundamental changes have been made over the centuries (52).

Those interested in working in this field will need to develop some additional skills, particularly in identifying and dating work according to its architectural style. A useful guide is *Recording a Church, An Illustrated Glossary* published by the CBA. The problems inherent in examining a large building will mean that you may have to seek permission to erect scaffolding or clamber around in towers or on roofs, all of which have safety implications. The best time to study a church in detail is during the course of major renovation. Scaffolding may be up already and in some cases the walls are laid bare prior to replastering. It is on such occasions that important discoveries can be made.

Another facet of church life that calls for study is the churchyard (53). As well as being an important feature of the landscape in its own right the graves that it contains are a vital record of family, social and art history. Unfortunately few stones will last for ever and as the years pass the inscriptions become less and less legible. There was also a movement in the 1960s to remove all the stones from a graveyard to tidy it up and make mowing easier! In the face of this destruction, many groups began surveying churchyards using as their guide the little book by Jeremy Jones, *How to Record Graveyards*, published by the CBA. Work begins with a careful mapping of the church to locate and identify the existing monuments and then record cards are completed for each stone. This data is ideally suited for computer analysis and programs have been written or adapted to serve this need. The work can stop at this point with the finished archive being copied and stored with the parish authorities, the local library and the Sites and Monuments Record. For those who wish to take the work further there are many conclusions that can be drawn from the evidence and written

52   The analysis of the fabric of a church based on a wall elevation. Not too many churches incorporate Roman walling but it does happen; this example is based on St Mary Northgate, Canterbury and the work of the Canterbury Archaeological Trust.

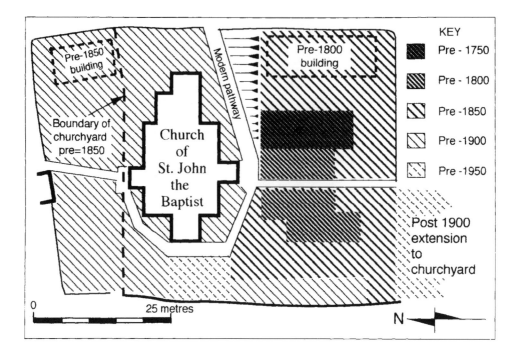

KEY

■	Pre - 1750
▨	Pre - 1800
▨	Pre -1850
▨	Pre -1900
▨	Pre -1950

Pre-1850 building

Pre-1800 building

Modern pathway

Boundary of churchyard pre=1850

Church of St. John the Baptist

Post 1900 extension to churchyard

0   25 metres

N

53 Bodicote, Oxfordshire. Plan of the churchyard drawn as part of a survey project by first-year students at Banbury School.

up. Work could be continued on the distribution by period and social group of graves in the churchyard. Another option could be to study the techniques of different stone masons and the changes in decorative style or lettering. Much of this work remains to be done with published surveys. Unfortunately there are a number of unfinished surveys lying about which need writing up. With the threat that seems to be hanging over some of the great municipal cemeteries, through privatization, these studies should perhaps be transferred also to more urban settings. The thought of beginning to record a cemetery which may have over a thousand nineteenth-century monuments is a rather daunting one; even so the work needs doing.

Fieldwalking

The techniques we have been looking at so far are non-destructive. When the job is completed there should be no mark to show that anything has been done and the site remains available to future workers. Excavation is the complete opposite of this for it destroys just about everything it touches. Fieldwalking represents a kind of half-way house, whilst not particularly destructive it is invasive as it can involve removing finds from the surface of ploughed fields. Once these finds have been removed they cannot be put back so the record is changed. Fieldwalking should not be undertaken casually.

Simply to go out and trawl through the fields for goodies, as some of the metal detector fraternity do, is irresponsible. Fieldwalking can only make sense if it is seen as part of a specific study, either of an area or of certain types of sites. It has to be done in an organized way and with the full co-operation of the landowner and the county archaeologist. If all these conditions are met, fieldwalking can be an extremely valuable tool in understanding the layout of existing sites and discovering new ones.

Some materials have an extended life within the plough soil and so are available for collecting. These include flint tools, flakes and cores, and building stone, tile and brick, some of the more robust types of pottery, and glass and metal artefacts. Few, if any, of these items will be of any significance in their own right but as part of a measured survey where their location is noted and their frequency counted they can become invaluable. The best time to be out is two or three weeks after the land has been ploughed. This will have allowed time for a certain amount of weathering which makes surface finds easier to pick out.

There are basically two styles of fieldwalking. The first is to satisfy the needs of a large-scale regional analysis. The aim may be to build up an overall picture of the pattern of human activity in your area. If this is so then you will need to walk every ploughed field either within a parish or inside a circle of, say, 2 km radius centring on your particular site. You cannot afford to look too intensely at every square metre, nor are you likely successfully to complete your work alone. The second style involves making a detailed investigation of a selected area or site and may involve just one or two fields with the aim of total collection of all items.

For an area study initial exploration can be conveniently done by walking the fields in a series of traverses. These should be regularly spaced and aligned with the National Grid (54). Once collecting starts on this scale it is becoming common practice to divide up the area into hectare squares (100 m a side) and further divide these up into eight runs of 25 by 50 m. Some time will have to be spent on the ground determining the location of the traverses with reference to the grid lines. These can be fixed by measuring along the hedge lines and marking the ends with canes or ranging rods. The limits of individual runs can then be located by sighting. Once the outlines are clear you

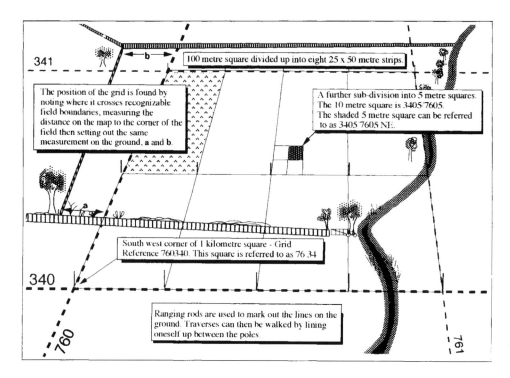

341

100 metre square divided up into eight 25 x 50 metre strips.

The position of the grid is found by noting where it crosses recognizable field boundaries, measuring the distance on the map to the corner of the field then setting out the same measurement on the ground, **a** and **b**.

A further sub-division into 5 metre squares. The 10 metre square is 3405/7605. The shaded 5 metre square can be referred to as 3405/7605 NE.

South west corner of 1 kilometre square - Grid Reference 760340. This square is referred to as 76 34

340

Ranging rods are used to mark out the lines on the ground. Traverses can then be walked by lining oneself up between the poles.

760

761

54 Using the National Grid to set out areas for collecting.

or your team can begin to search. Within these areas all finds are collected and saved in labelled bags. Large resealable plastic freezer bags are frequently used, although if finds come in large quantities or are unusually heavy then stout brown paper bags or even labelled buckets may have to be used. The labels should include information about the site, the number of the run and the date.

For sites where a more detailed picture is called for the size of the grid is reduced to enable collection to be carried out in 5 m squares. Obviously the number of individual bags will proliferate as will the problem of recording which square is which. Again the National Grid comes to the rescue: as each hectare square will have its own unique reference the 5 m squares within it can similarly be identified by combinations of numbers.

Once the finds have been removed from the site the next step is to wash them and begin to analyse what has turned up. Having discarded items of natural origin the material will have to be sorted into groups. Some finds such as building materials may simply be weighed and counted then set aside. Pottery will need to be identified by type and

82

period and then rebagged with a new descriptive label; these fragments too will be weighed and counted. Some pieces of pottery which are especially important for diagnostic purposes may be individually labelled and bagged, making sure that references to the original find spot are kept intact. Certain articles, such as flint tools or metalwork, may demand further study and preservation.

For the beginner the variety of different pottery types and fabrics can be bewildering. Unfortunately there are no short cuts to learning about pottery. It is simply a case of building up experience by handling as much of it as you can that comes from known datable sources. Visits to museums and especially their reserve collections are probably the best way to build up a picture of the kinds of ware you will be likely to come across in your area. Even so it may be necessary to turn to the museum staff for a suitable specialist to help identify the more obscure pieces that turn up.

The next step is to draw out a site plan with your collecting grid superimposed so you can plot the comparative densities of the different categories of find you are interested in. These are conventionally shown by circles within each square and tied into specific amounts with a key (55). As with any distribution map scatters of surface finds have to be interpreted with care. Much of what is found on the fields in the way of domestic debris has been spread as part of the practice of manuring which goes back to prehistoric times. Building materials can be useful indicators of the existence of certain types of structure but even they can become distributed across an area through the action of the plough.

When all the work is complete you will need to find a permanent home for copies of your plans, diagrams and notes and again the Sites and Monuments people will probably be happy to take them on. If individual items of interest have been discovered you may have to liaise between the landowner and the local museum with a view to ensuring their preservation. While museums will have space for some items collected they certainly will not want to have custody of every fragment of pot, tile or brick that has come up so they must be disposed of carefully. Some articles recovered from fieldwalking have found their way into 'handling kits' prepared for schools. These give the children a chance to examine and sort and classify materials from a known historical context. If you do need to throw things away you should do so in a way which will not cause confusion to later generations of fieldworkers. This means not spreading them across your back garden. Perhaps the safest way to dispose of unwanted material is to deposit it at a public landfill site where it will be securely buried with plenty of late twentieth-century rubbish!

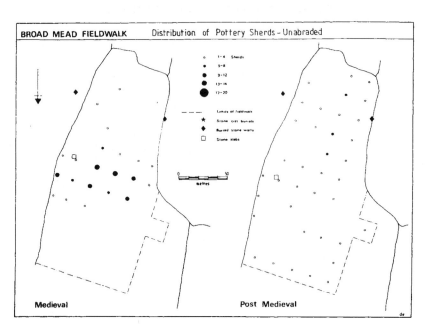

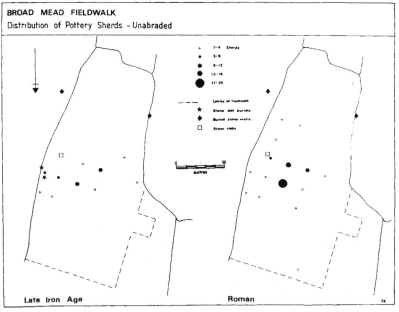

84

Organization and management

55 The analysis of fieldwalking data, from Blashenwell Farm, Dorset.

Although your first experience of orchestrated fieldwork will probably be as a helper on an investigation that someone else has started this section describes how it is possible to set up a project from scratch and underlines some of the organizational tasks that have to be taken on. From the very beginning it is important to have a clear set of aims and objectives in mind so that you can give a clear account of your intentions to any interested parties. There is considerable freedom of choice for those working independently; however, it is only sensible to find out as much as possible about local needs. It would be hard to justify a detailed study of non-threatened sites when people were working just down the road to survey the route of a new motorway.

If you had a particular interest in water-mills your overall aim might be to investigate mill sites in your county so as to supplement existing source materials and encourage a more positive attitude towards their preservation. A detailed list of objectives might read:

1 To investigate all known existing mills with particular reference to their state of preservation and future prospects.
2 To choose one or two threatened sites for detailed investigation and recording.
3 To search for mill sites by a combination of map work and field-walking with particular reference to those mills listed in Domesday Book.
4 To produce a gazetteer of all mill sites discovered.
5 To publish a booklet on the subject for the general public locally, which includes notes for mill owners on their preservation.
6 To plan and set up in conjunction with the county museum an exhibition of the work done.

This is clearly a large undertaking which could involve a dozen or more people working most weekends and some holidays over a period of a couple of years (56). A smaller scale undertaking might involve making a record of milestones in your area. The general aim would be that such a record be made; the contributory objectives might be to identify their locations from maps, visit each one and photograph it, present a portfolio of pictures and background notes to the county SMR and send an outline copy of your findings to the highways department with a plea that they treat these minor monuments with some respect in their road improvement schemes! Two or three people could complete this in a year.

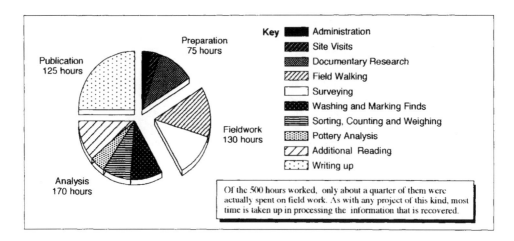

Key
Administration
Site Visits
Documentary Research
Field Walking
Surveying
Washing and Marking Finds
Sorting, Counting and Weighing
Pottery Analysis
Additional Reading
Writing up

Preparation
75 hours

Publication
125 hours

Fieldwork
130 hours

Analysis
170 hours

Of the 500 hours worked, only about a quarter of them were actually spent on field work. As with any project of this kind, most time is taken up in processing the information that is recovered.

56 Blashenwell Farm Project, allocation of time.

A popular focus for research over the past few years has been the parish survey. This has often been organized as an evening class with some of the findings being fed into the Sites and Monuments Record with other details being written into a parish history or exhibited for the community. Parish surveys can vary in their approach but often contain a sizeable chunk of local history alongside the archaeology, so there is plenty to do for those who do not enjoy getting muddy.

In setting up such an investigation you will almost certainly need to consult widely at the planning stage. You will need to know what work has already been done. Is there a specialist in the field who can offer guidance and advice? Is there sufficient interest around to make it a viable undertaking? If you are working under the umbrella of a local society you will have to judge the strength of the suppport they can offer, is there hard cash available or just the use of their name?

Funding is an important question as there is bound to be some investment called for. The participants are likely to transport themselves around but do you need to buy extra equipment? Who will pay for films and drawing materials? What about the cost of any publications? Grants are occasionally available for field study projects from some of the larger societies, and Lloyds bank has for many years made funds available for small groups to buy equipment. You might make some progress in seeking commercial sponsorship locally if you believe your project may have some publicity value. Again you could capitalize on the educational potential by linking up with a local school or college who might be able to make a contribution. Remember that gifts in kind can be almost as useful as money.

Something will have to be done about assembling the equipment you will need and storing it when not in use. Even basic items such as a good 30 m tape will not be cheap and some pieces such as optical levels can cost several hundred pounds. The responsibilities for care and maintenance should be clearly set out. Some thought needs to be given to personnel matters. What structures will there be for managing the project? Will you work collectively or will a project supervisor be selected? Do further areas of responsibility need to be defined or will everyone wade in to do a bit here and a bit there? Remember that an enterprise that starts off on a wave of enthusiasm can founder after a few months of gruelling fieldwork as people's energy starts to wane. Clear agreed aims and strong positive leadership will do much to avoid the doldrums yet even so any project should have a fall back position of perhaps somewhat reduced objectives should support fail. The most demanding management role when working with large parties will be that of co-ordinating everyone's efforts. If small groups are going out to survey individual sites a record needs to be kept of who has been where to avoid duplication of effort. Equally, if everyone is needed for a major piece of fieldwalking one weekend someone has to take responsibility for getting everyone together and informing them all if for some reason the outing has to be called off.

You will need to adopt some common policy on methods and

57 A standard record card for use in an earthwork survey project. It was devised for a survey of recent damage inflicted on round barrows in an area around Poole in Dorset.

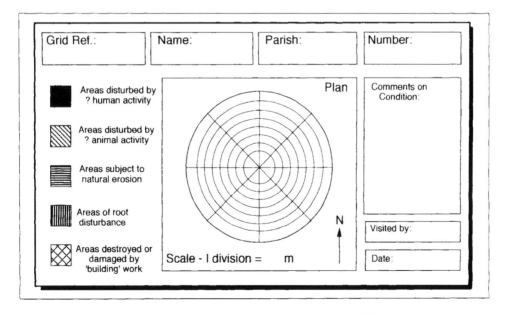

Grid Ref.:	Name:	Parish:	Number:

Areas disturbed by ? human activity

Areas disturbed by ? animal activity

Areas subject to natural erosion

Areas of root disturbance

Areas destroyed or damaged by 'building' work

Plan

Comments on Condition:

N

Scale - I division =   m

Visited by:

Date:

conventions for recording data (57). This is particularly important if several sub-groups are working at different locations or if the project is likely to go on for several years and must therefore accommodate people coming and going. The adoption of standard forms and a standard vocabulary will simplify matters. Well-used examples include the field card produced by the Moated Sites Research Group, *A Systematic Procedure for Recording English Vernacular Architecture* published by the Ancient Monuments Society, and the recording system outlined in *How To Record Graveyards* by Jeremy Jones, published by the CBA. Many of the special interest groups listed in Appendix 1 will have developed procedures which may be relevant for your use. If not, have a look at what is around and then make your own up.

Someone will have to be responsible for negotiating the permissions necessary before survey work can begin. It is one thing to collect a casual, 'Yes I'm sure it will be OK' to an equally casual request to take a quick look at a site, but if a large number of people are going to be at work over several days things have to be sorted out more thoroughly. The first step is to approach the landowner or their accredited agent. This is not easy, especially out in the countryside: many farmers are tenants and the real owners of the land may be hidden behind a whole series of agents and holding companies. If you are unable to get through to the actual owner you must make sure that the person you do deal with can speak with authority. There is nothing quite so embarrassing as being in charge of a group which is unceremoniously ejected from a property because the right person was not approached. Permission should be obtained in writing whenever possible. If you are intending to collect and carry away finds from ploughed surfaces you must remember that this material is normally the property of the landowner. The only exception is in the case of treasure trove which belongs to the Crown. Although the owner will not be too disappointed to see you carting away buckets full of pottery or tile fragments it will be a different matter if coins or other potentially valuable finds come up. If you can agree in advance what the ultimate fate of material found will be, particularly in terms of depositing important finds with a museum, then all should be well.

As the fieldwork nears its end there ought to be a clear route mapped out through analysis and research to final publication (58). Many small-scale endeavours never get written up effectively and fewer still are published. Part of the problem is that it is difficult to write by committee. Often one or two individuals will take on responsibility for publication and the others leave them to it. Then some vital member of the group will move away, taking their notes, and suddenly the whole thing starts

58 Organization of a fieldwork project, Blashenwell Farm.

88

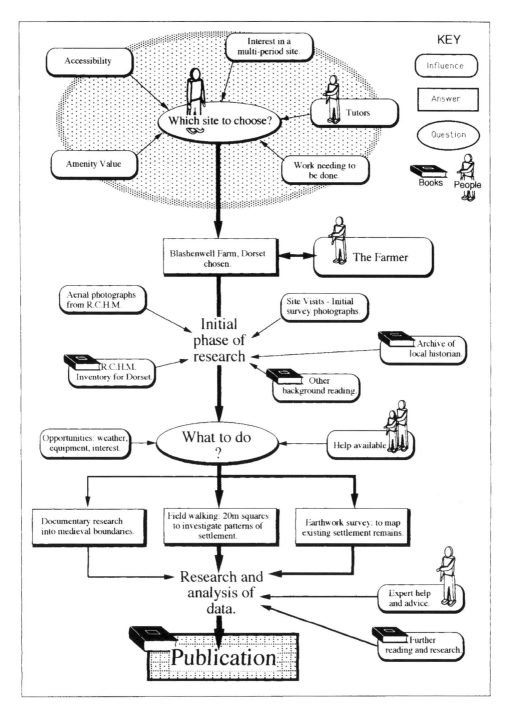

KEY

Influence

Answer

Question

Books   People

Which site to choose?

Accessibility

Interest in a multi-period site.

Tutors

Amenity Value

Work needing to be done.

Blashenwell Farm, Dorset chosen.

The Farmer

Aerial photographs from R.C.H.M.

Site Visits - Initial survey photographs.

Initial phase of research

Archive of local historian.

R.C.H.M. Inventory for Dorset.

Other background reading.

What to do ?

Opportunities: weather, equipment, interest.

Help available

Documentary research into medieval boundaries.

Field walking: 20m squares to investigate patterns of settlement.

Earthwork survey: to map existing settlement remains.

Research and analysis of data.

Expert help and advice.

Publication

Further reading and research.

to fall apart. The answer is to plan in such a way that the presentation of results becomes as exciting as the initial fieldwork. Preparing an exhibition or a day for schools or a press launch of a finished report can help keep the group together and give additional support and deadlines to those who are struggling with the writing up.

Publication

All archaeologists are under an obligation to communicate the results of their studies. This is particularly so where some measure of 'destruction' has been caused, as in fieldwalking. Information can be passed on through lectures, seminars or exhibitions but the best permanent record is in a publication of some kind. If you have been working under the aegis of a society then the automatic route to publication should be through their proceedings. It is important not to confuse the kind of interim notes that they may publish with the final record. Interim notes exist simply to bring people up to date with what you are doing. Unfortunately they remain the only published reference to all too many projects.

If you have secured an agreement to publish from your local society you will need to liaise closely with their editor and be meticulous in observing the various conventions asked of you. This will affect the way the manuscript is typed, and the format and size of any diagrams or plans you want to include. Unless they are being very generous with separate folders or pull-out plans, much of your work will have to be reduced to fit the printed page. You will probably have to redraw some of your material to a suitable format for reduction, remembering to remove any fine detail which will be lost or blurred during reduction and increasing the size of any captions so they can be read comfortably. You can best get a feel for what is wanted by studying similar pieces that have been published in earlier years.

The normal layout for a published paper is to begin with a description of why and where the work was done and what methods were used, this is followed by the detail of the results obtained and some analysis of their meaning and wider significance. An overall conclusion will sum up, followed by acknowledgements and a bibliography. You should be scrupulously fair in acknowledging all the help you have received from archaeologists and non-archaeologists alike. Many journals will ask for a brief resumé or summary of the paper to be printed alongside it for those who want to know if they are going to be interested in your piece!

If you are unable to place your work in a journal then you will need to explore other avenues. Sometimes the local museums service will be prepared to publish important work as an occasional paper, or if you think there is a link you may be able to persuade a local company to take it on through their in-house publishing network. If all else fails there is no reason at all why you should not publish it yourself. In this era of desk-top publishing, colour photocopiers and cheap corner print shops there is no sensible excuse for work remaining unpublished. In this case it is not getting the work printed that is the problem, the problem now is distribution. You will need to guarantee the long-term survival of your work by sending copies to any bodies who may be interested in holding a copy. Libraries, museums, university departments and county archaeologists and units are all possibilities. You certainly ought to be able to sell some copies either by advertising in the archaeological press or persuading your local museum and bookshops to have copies on sale or return. Finally get the local paper to interview you about the work and make sure you put in a plug for your publication together with details of where it can be obtained.

4 Joining an excavation

Fieldwork and excavation

In the course of developing your understanding of the landscape and the human activities that contributed towards it you will come across many features that despite your best efforts remain unexplained. We have seen how survey techniques for measuring earthworks, or collecting pottery from the fields, begin to fill in pieces of the jigsaw that makes up the past. Special techniques such as aerial photography and geophysical surveys provide a few more pieces but there has always been a feeling that the full picture can only be revealed by excavation. Indeed, there was a time when archaeologists said things like 'this problem can only be solved by excavation'. Excavation not only solves problems, it also creates them. Logistics, management, data handling and conservation will present their own difficulties and more questions. To top all this comes the reminder that excavation, rather like the dissection of anatomical specimens, destroys the very evidence it sets out to examine.

Despite this, excavation remains a popular activity. It enables the archaeologist to indulge fully his or her curiosity about what went on at a given site. Of course this inquisitiveness is disciplined by being indulged in within an academic framework as part of a scientific investigation. This becomes important later on when we consider issues such as site discipline. Excavation also serves other purposes within the archaeological community.

Some excavations are opened for reasons which are 'political' in nature. This might reflect national politics as when a need is seen to investigate some great national monument. Local politics can sometimes influence the course of excavation as in the case of the new towns who want ancient monuments exposed to give a sense of identity to their communities. Then there are office politics. Some archaeologists have a living to earn and a career to think of which will involve them in a certain amount of competition for the best jobs. In these circumstances a successful series of excavations is a very public way of establishing a reputation.

Most excavations are major social events, they bring together a variety of people from different backgrounds to work together. This human mix can prove to be fertile intellectual ground for generating new ideas and re-examining old ones. Ideas may arise from the kind of cross-fertilization that happens when experts from different specializations come together on site. A particular instance of this was the way a butcher's apprentice working as a volunteer transformed everyone's ideas as to what it meant to cut up a carcass! The combination of communal living, limited facilities and long dull periods when nothing much seems to be happening produces a climate where it is easy to get to know people very well, very quickly. Once a dig gets into its second or third season an element of reunion enters the picture so that some excavations of long standing come to resemble family outings.

There is still a sense, despite what has been written in the first three chapters, that digging is what archaeology is really about. It is what the public expect archaeologists to do. Archaeologists have increasingly been resisting pressures to dig and have explored alternatives to excavation. The recent controversy over whether or not to resume digging at Sutton Hoo showed this process in action. However, there is still an unspoken belief that fieldwork is a kind of second best, something safe and suited to local societies and evening classes while the real masters get on and dig. Fortunately there are a number of younger archaeologists who are currently doing a lot to redress the balance so that fieldwork is no longer seen as a poor relation.

The degree of destruction involved, the implications under employment law and health and safety legislation are such that excavation should never be embarked on unsupported or unsupervised. The organization of a dig, the interpretation of what is uncovered and its eventual publication are all heavy responsibilities. Only those with considerable experience and plenty of back-up can shoulder them. However, that experience can be gained over a period of years and new diggers can feel confident that with an open and enquiring approach they can begin to develop their own expertise.

Although individual excavations are to be strongly discouraged, experience gained during digging can be useful at other times. With the amount of building that is going on it is quite impossible for professional archaeologists to maintain a watching brief on all sites. In these circumstances the presence of a trained observer can be invaluable

59 Keeping a careful eye on pipe-laying operations in the Abbey Meadows, Redditch.

in sounding warning bells should anything interesting start to come up. While large-scale developments will almost certainly have taken archaeological advice there are many operations such as pipe-laying (59), road widening and small building jobs which need an eye keeping on them. The key to success is to maintain good relationships, both with the workers on site and with the county archaeology team, so that action can be taken quickly if necessary.

Making preparations

As a new volunteer the beginner can expect to spend a couple of weeks of hard work in all weathers. What rewards can there possibly be to make up for these privations? Firstly you will have your curiosity satisfied, as each fresh bucket of spoil is removed from the site a pattern will unfold in front of you. It does help, as Philip Rahtz has remarked, if you actually enjoy moving large quantities of dirt. There will be opportunities to learn new skills from sharpening scythes to driving mechanical excavators. There will be the satisfaction that comes from making a contribution to a real team effort and at the end of the day you may even find yourself leaner and fitter. You will certainly make new friends and quite possibly influence people. Supervisors and directors should always be willing to listen to well thought out ideas about what is going on in your corner of the dig. Although finding objects is not the be-all-and-end-all of archaeology nobody can pretend that they do not enjoy a quiet thrill when something nice comes up. Finally, if you are fortunate, you may get paid and so take home an additional financial reward.

There are a number of ways to find out about excavations which need volunteer help. The starting point for national coverage is, as already mentioned, the CBA's *British Archaeological News* and its calendar of excavations. This lists digs by location and includes information about the period the site belongs to, who is organizing the work, what the requirements are for workers and what is likely to be provided on site in the way of domestic comforts. The newsletter comes out six times a year and is only available by subscription (£10 for 1991). *Current Archaeology* has also begun printing supplements which list excavations where help is needed. Some excavations advertise in the national press while others may feature locally. Many societies still do dig themselves or support the activities of their local unit or county archaeologist. If you want to work close to home they would certainly be the best people to approach first. For more adventurous spirits wanting to work abroad there is the Archaeology Abroad Service run as a non-profit-making organization based at the Institute of Archaeology in London. Their bulletins listing opportunities to dig overseas are issued three times a year to subscribers. General advice, however, is that it is inadvisable to work abroad until some experience of basic digging has been obtained here.

If it comes to making a choice of which excavation to apply to it may help to consider what kind of dig you would enjoy most. There are three main types, rescue, research and training although there can be some overlap between these different categories.

Rescue excavations

Rescue excavations arise in response to some particular threat. Increasingly these are run in agreement with the developers which means that the drama of snatching evidence away from the very jaws of the JCB is less common than it was. Rescue work will now take place over several weeks or even months before the contractors move in. Despite this the working conditions can still be difficult, the hours long and the pressure to get results considerable. There is also a cheerful disregard for the normal summer digging season. There are fewer openings for

60 A 'rescue' dig. Excavating a barrow on Twyford Down, Hampshire in advance of the M3.

volunteers in this kind of operation and little time for training. On the other hand there have been cases when particularly urgent projects have relied on local labour who have enjoyed the sense of excitement and challenge that rescue work brings (60).

Research digs

Research digs will be the ones most commonly advertised. Some may be one-off projects while others may have been running for many years to the point where they have developed their own 'culture'. The standards of excavation and recording are likely to be high and the academic background may be formidable. Most such digs will take inexperienced volunteers but training can be sporadic and poorly co-ordinated. This is not always the case, but you must be prepared to ask for help should you feel out of touch with what is going on. The great advantages to such work are the freedom to progress at a pace which allows time for reflection and debate, the chances to work on major sites with well-known archaeologists and the opportunity to employ 'state of the art' techniques and equipment.

Training digs

Training digs represent the main entry point for those new to archae-ology. Several universities run their own primarily for undergraduates although other trainees are welcomed, providing they can meet the cost. Paying for training is fine provided it is of a high quality. There have been one or two instances in the past where directors have taken the money and used the luckless volunteers as labourers. If you intend to pay for training you should obtain in advance notice of what activities you will be engaged on. Instruction should be partly 'on the job' and partly through lectures and seminars. It would be reasonable to expect the course to include information about the site, its background and the chief periods you are likely to be dealing with. There should also be training in the use of basic hand tools and experience of the day-to-day recording system. Additional instruction may be provided for activities such as plan and section drawing and the use of specialist survey equipment, or basic finds handling and conservation (**61**).

The character of an excavation will also depend on the kind of organization running it. Some societies run small-scale excavations which only take place at weekends. Others will be conducting major pieces of research with several weeks of continuous digging. Whatever the case, society-run digs are usually amongst the most friendly; after all, their existence depends on the continuing support of their members.

61 Dr Grenville Astill giving an on-site lecture on the industrial site at Bordesley Abbey.

They are generally well used to introducing beginners to the intricacies of excavation.

The local units and some of the national societies can vary in their approach to volunteers. Many have played down the role of local volunteers and relied on teams of professional diggers. Some units have woken up to the importance of involving communities and are making fresh efforts to employ local people, so this may change. The nature of university-based excavations depends on whether the dig is primarily for training or research purposes. As we have seen, formal training usually has to be paid for whereas an individual having to run his or her project on a limited budget will generally welcome assistance.

Other factors may well influence your choice of site. You may have a strong interest in a particular period, although single period sites are something of a rarity. As your experience grows you may be attracted to a name and want to work with an individual you may have heard of or read about. The distinctions between urban and rural sites can be quite significant. Working in the country you will be able to enjoy a fairly peaceful atmosphere, and perhaps an attractive setting, but facilities will be limited. In a town or city you will have every convenience around you as well as all the noise and litter. In the countryside accommodation is usually in tents or caravans, in towns you may have to make your own arrangements or bed down in a church hall or hostel (62).

62　Resting on the camp site during a lunch break.

One final factor which may affect the type of excavation you sign up for is the nature of the sub-soil! On a multi-period urban site this is not quite so relevant as the occupation will have built up its own local environment. Elsewhere clay, chalk, gravel and peat will all have an impact on the kind of digging you will do. Clay is difficult to work on when it is dry and impossible in the wet. In dry conditions it hardens and cracks and loses colour; in the wet it sticks and smears and cannot be walked on. Features dug into clay, and then refilled with clay, take some excavating; yet preservation of finds, especially in waterlogged conditions, can be very good and stratification deep.

Sites on chalk often lack deep stratification for various reasons relating to location and land use; the excavator is often faced with just the bottoms of post-holes, ditches and gullies left in place. Having said this, few things stand out as clearly as features cut into chalk. Newly exposed chalk can be quite wearing to work on in bright weather and diggers do sometimes complain of the glare thrown back from the surface. While it always seems to be raining on clay sites, chalk sites are always windy!

Despite the fact that many important prehistoric remains are found on gravel it has few admirers as a material on which to work. Its extremely abrasive nature leads to bloodied knuckles and tools that wear out after only a few weeks of use. Gravel sites are also characterized by huge featureless expanses where nothing ever happens and the endless thrum of heavy machinery working somewhere just out of sight.

Working on peat and related materials has given birth to a whole school of 'wetland' archaeology. As the name suggests wetness is the order of the day. In order to maintain the astonishing degree of preservation of organic remains such sites are often kept permanently sprayed with water so that the excavators hardly ever really dry out either. To contrast with this, on moorland areas, where the peat can dry out, conditions become highly acidic and not a lot of anything survives except granite and gold.

Once you have selected a site on which to try your hand the next step is to write to whoever is dealing with recruitment. On all but the largest sites this will probably be the director. You should ask for full details and an application form enclosing a self-addressed stamped envelope. The kind of documentation you are likely to receive should include an interim note describing work on the site last year or an outline of the research brief for a new dig. There also ought to be a sheet of information about domestic matters and perhaps a map of how to get there. An application form will ask for personal details such as name, address, date of birth and any particular health problems or dietary requirements. You are also likely to be asked about any previous experience or special skills you might have so that the director can have some idea of the aptitude of the team that is being assembled.

Assuming that your application is successful and you have a starting date, what next? One essential requirement for anyone going on an excavation is that their anti-tetanus protection is up to date. You should check this with your doctor if unsure. As there is no such thing as a typical excavation the notes that follow are based on what you might find on a medium-sized research dig organized by a university department on a rural site. You will probably have had to make your own way to the site which could have been a problem if you were relying on public transport. Many excavations in remote areas will run a mini-bus service to the nearest bus stop or station when people are arriving or leaving.

You will be responsible for your own accommodation. This means the first thing you will want to do on arrival is put up your tent. Around the camp site you should expect to find a source of water suitable for washing and drinking. Washing facilities may be spartan or non-existent. The chances are that the toilets on site will be of the chemical variety and emptying them and topping them up with fresh 'Elsan Blue' will be a regular chore for someone. There may be camp management duties which could involve you in a variety of tasks that ensure the camp site and other domestic arrangements function effectively. Other jobs might include emptying litter bins and washing up after meals.

Most excavations offer some kind of communal catering which may operate on a rota basis; although large digs will often employ one or two full-time cooks. There will probably be some kind of large shelter, a marquee or barn or church hall which is used as a dining hall, common room and lecture theatre. As well as the digging there will probably be some lectures and possibly field trips to other sites, but there will still be some time at the end of the day for socializing or just reading a book. There is a tradition of ending a long day's work with an evening in the local pub.

The question foremost in everyone's mind when they first approach a new dig is 'will I be made welcome?' The answer is 'yes', with some qualification. Most people arriving on site will be new to each other so there is an inevitable period of getting to know everyone. On the other hand there may be people who have been before or who form part of the staff who already constitute a social group. If it bothers you, you might want to organize your own group in advance by talking a friend into accompanying you. Some people do believe that there is an innate hostility between professional excavators and amateur volunteers. I think it may happen but when it does it has more to do with personal differences rather than questions of status. If you should ever encounter that kind of snobbishness remember that you have been accepted by the director as part of a team and your contribution is as valuable as anyone else's.

It is very hard to be more specific about these kinds of details as they vary so much from site to site. The best advice is to find out as much as you can in advance and be prepared. You may find yourself having to rough it or you could be housed in luxury in the wing of a great country house, as long as you know what to expect you should have no cause for complaint. Most excavations run smoothly on both the domestic and archaeological fronts but unfortunately not all good archaeologists have the time to be good managers too. Some get around this by appointing a camp manager as a separate post to leave them clear to concentrate on the digging. It is to them that the queries or complaints about domestic arrangements should first be addressed. However, final responsibility for all aspects of the dig rests with the director who should listen sympathetically to any unresolved problems. It is in everyone's interests to see that volunteers are happy and healthy. If a reasoned appeal does not do the trick remember you are not working in a prison camp; feel free to take your labour elsewhere.

Looking after yourself

The safety record of British archaeology, at least in terms of fatalities, is a good one. Less satisfying is the number of minor injuries which occur on a regular basis. The frequency with which bruises, grazes and sprains are suffered indicates that there are still cases of poor site management and personal irresponsibility. The legal framework is set out in the 1974 Health and Safety at Work Act. This imposes a duty of care on both employers and employees for safety around the work place. It is important to note that even an unpaid volunteer may be considered an employee under the terms of the act which also covers the safety of visitors to the site. As far as the individual digger is concerned he or she finds him or herself at the sharp end of this legislation. While the director and supervisors have a responsibility not to institute unsafe practices, each worker should ensure through vigilance and personal good conduct that dangerous practices are avoided.

This sense of taking care of yourself begins with turning up for work in suitable clothing. Sound footwear needs to be worn when working with or near heavy hand tools such as pickaxes or forks. Well-fitting boots with steel toe-caps are best. One might expect that this point would not need emphasizing, yet every year there are a number of painful injuries that result from people doing heavy labour in training shoes or even sandals. Ordinary wellington boots offer no protection at all, although strengthened versions can be bought that could be useful on some sites. Boots should be worn with good quality thick woollen socks or else the chafing that can result can be just as disabling as any other foot injury. Lighter weight footwear such as training shoes are appropriate wear on a dry site where no heavy digging is being done. Slip on sandals, being both insecure in their grip and insubstantial in the support they offer, should be left on the beach.

In fine weather many diggers prefer to wear shorts and are prepared to put up with the odd graze for the sake of comfort. If you are trowelling in shorts you might want to invest in knee pads or the kind of kneeling mat that gardeners use. Denim jeans as work trousers seem pretty well standard but they offer little comfort in the wet. Looser trousers in a thick fabric like corduroy will not cling in the same way and will dry out faster. Different varieties and combinations of T-shirts, sweat shirts and jumpers should be worn on the well established principle that in poor weather it is best to wear a number of layers of clothing. These can be added to or removed as the temperature and the activities change. If you do decide to expose a lot of bare skin to the sun do remember that you are likely to be out at work for far longer than the average sunbather spends on the beach. It is very easy to become involved in the work and forget the damage that is being done to your skin until you try and climb into your sleeping bag at night. Because of the penetrative powers of ultraviolet radiation sunburn can occur even on cloudy days.

There are some jobs, such as shifting rubble, where a strong pair of gardening or work gloves is essential. Otherwise it is really a matter of personal preference. There is no doubt that decent gloves reduce the number of cuts and grazes a digger receives, do something to alleviate the problem of blisters and keep your hands free of ingrained dirt. If you do use gloves have a spare pair around, with regular use on site they can soon wear out.

Of all the precautions that can be taken to avoid serious injury the wearing of a hard hat is the most effective. They are available from most DIY outlets and are not expensive. They will need some adjustment to be made to fit snugly on your head as per the instructions inside. Hard hats should be worn by everyone who is working with or near large hand tools such as picks or forks and by anyone working on or close to mechanical excavators. Any person working in a way that puts their head below the level of any passers-by should also wear one. This means that even trowellers working on the edge of an excavated area or next to a barrow run should consider protection for their heads against a dropped bucket or an overturned barrow. There are people who seem to think that it in some way compromises their 'strong man' image to wear a safety helmet. They are fools.

When the sun is shining a broad-brimmed hat not only shades the eyes, it can also prevent serious sunburn to the back of the neck. By contrast, in cold conditions much of the body's heat can be lost through the top of the head so the addition of a cap or woolly hat can keep you warmer. There may be occasions when extra protection is called for eyes, ears, nose and throat. Using a pick on pebbly ground can create a risk from flying splinters of stone and so safety glasses or goggles become a necessity. Sun-glasses offer good protection to the eyes from glare and dust but they reduce your ability to distinguish colours on the ground; eye shades may be the favoured option. Ear defenders should be supplied if you have to work close to noisy machinery, while on certain sites where dust is a problem face masks can be issued. Workers excavating on the site of the Roman baths at Bath had to wear similar masks as protection against a parasitic amoeba but this kind of hazard is comparatively rare.

63 Excavating can mean a long time spent in an uncomfortable position.

Good working practices also make a major contribution to health and safety on site. Tools should always be stored safely when not in use, neatly stacked so that any sharp edges or points are in the ground and not lying ready for the unwary to step on. There are times when there are so many assorted lines and pegs around the site that it resembles an obstacle course and tripping over them can be a common occurrence. You can help yourself by remaining aware of what is going on around you, but it is also the responsibility of the supervisors to make sure that everyone knows as new lines are put up and to ensure access routes are as uncluttered as possible.

Smoking on site is rarely allowed, partly for the offence it is likely to cause to other diggers, and partly because of the risk of contamination from cigarette ash. Most excavations will frown on radios being played. Unnecessary noise interferes with other people's concentration and can contribute to the confusion if an accident does happen and action is called for. Similarly personal stereos are a barrier to communication whether it is a request for information or a cry for help. Rowdy behaviour is always discouraged as it increases the probability that an accident will occur and in any case it is just not an appropriate part of a scientific investigation.

In deep excavations a very strict set of rules, listed in the various sets of statutory construction regulations, come into play. These are too complex to summarize here but obviously they are designed to guard against the risk of the sides of the trench collapsing. Putting in suitable shoring needs the attention of a skilled technician. Access is likely to be by ladder and there may be hoists, pumps and other specialist equipment in use. All in all this is not the ideal working environment for the casual volunteer. If you are asked to work in these conditions make sure that you know and understand what is required of you and if you are not happy working in a deep excavation then ask to be moved somewhere else.

The volunteer has a responsibility to turn up on site in good general health. As well as being protected against tetanus this also means being free from infection. If you have got, or have just recovered from, an infectious disease, particularly a gastro-intestinal infection, then you should stay at home. Excavations have been all but closed down by epidemics following the arrival of a person suffering from a 'mild tummy bug'! Most excavations will have an established link with local health-care facilities and should be prepared to help you should you fall ill during the dig but as always, the best cure is prevention and on an excavation this means scrupulous attention to personal hygiene. Every separate part of an excavation needs its own well-equipped first-aid box and the presence of a qualified first-aider. Even so an accident may well occur and the responsibility for coping with it may well be yours! It is in your own interest to make some attempt to acquire relevant skills, enquiries to the local branch of the Red Cross or Saint John Ambulance Brigade should prove useful.

Because the volunteer is likely to be working out of doors for long periods in a variety of weather conditions it is important to be aware of the effects that exposure to the different extremes of climate can have. Hot weather can lead to a number of problems of increasing degrees of severity from sunburn, to heat exhaustion to sunstroke. Sunburn will show up as red and tender patches on the skin, perhaps with some blistering. Heat exhaustion happens because of the loss of salt and water from the body. Its symptoms are headaches, dizziness and nausea with muscular cramps. Heatstroke is a different condition brought about when the body's temperature rises out of control. The casualty will feel hot and restless and look flushed although the skin is dry. The pulse may begin to race and unconsciousness result. All of these conditions can be serious and may need proper medical advice.

At the other extreme cold weather can lead to exposure and hypothermia. The temperature does not have to be particularly low for these conditions to arise. Exhaustion, wet clothes and high altitude can all lead to a fall in body temperature to a dangerously low level. Symptoms include the body feeling cold to the touch, uncontrollable shivering, poor muscle co-ordination, and slurred or irrational speech. Treatment before removal to hospital is designed to prevent any further loss of heat and warm the body gently. Casualties should be placed under shelter and any additional garments or insulation used to cover them. Hot sweet drinks may be given but never alcohol.

Making observations

One of the most important reasons for joining an excavation is curiosity about the past within the disciplined framework of a scientific investigation. This idea is an important one when we look at personal conduct and individual responsibility during the course of a dig. A well-run, well-balanced excavation can be a very funny place, the humour ranging from the quietly witty to the hilarious. However, there is an underlying seriousness of purpose that the archaeologist never loses sight of. In accepting a place on an excavation the volunteer is also accepting the disciplines that unite all scientists and scholars in the basic principles of academic integrity. These are a respect for evidence, a determination to work hard to advance the research, a willingness to share new ideas and information, and a respect for the work of other individuals.

As far as the beginner is concerned the best advice is probably to watch what goes on and learn by example. Most supervisors will organize their work force in such a way that the experienced and the inexperienced work side by side. Although there is a place for formal training most excavators have learnt their craft as apprentices. The majority of individuals are usually only too pleased to take on a trainee to whom they can show off their skills.

One of the best diggers I ever knew was a farmer. Apart from being well suited to the work in terms of his physique he was also an extremely practical individual and understood the physical reality of events. He knew what was involved in digging ditches or erecting posts, he had seen what had happened to the old barn that was being allowed to collapse slowly and appreciated what was involved in patching a hole in the farmyard with whatever materials were around. Because he had a firm grip on practicalities of these activities he could look at the archaeological record and draw specific parallels with his own experience. Of course we cannot all have access to that range of activities but we can come close by looking and learning as we go around.

64 Iron Age fort reconstructed? The cross-country course at Gatcombe Park.

Experimental archaeologists do this kind of thing systematically, by burying dead pigs and digging them up again, building timber huts then burning them down and by recording in meticulous detail the contents of dustbins and the articles left behind in an abandoned farmhouse. For the rest of us this kind of information is freely available to a keen observer. If you are working on an excavation of an industrial site visit one of the museums where they have working displays and study the rubbish on the floor. Visit a stone mason at work on a church restoration project before trying to understand how a medieval church was built. Interested in timber fortifications? Try visiting one of the major cross-country courses used for horse trials. There you will find banks, ditches, revetments and palisades a-plenty (64).

The making of these kinds of contemporary observations (65) is sometimes called ethnoarchaeology. The study can be given an additional impetus by visiting other countries where practices long abandoned at home can still be seen to flourish abroad. Insights into the layout of Iron Age communities in Britain came from studying Kenyan villages. There are only a handful of primitive horizontal-wheeled water-mills to be found in the far north of Britain but there are hundreds in northern Spain. As an archaeologist you will interpret discoveries in the light of your own experience. The wider that experience is the less likely you are to be fooled into the assumption that all people at all times shared our western twentieth-century values.

An additional window on the past can come through archival photographs (66). The pace of change has increased enormously during the second half of the twentieth century. Prior to this many practices, especially in areas such as farming, had remained unchanged for centuries and had lingered on long enough for them to be photographed.

Because excavation is a communal undertaking social skills are also important. You will have to work alongside a number of people as part of a team. The most common instance of this will be when you are trowelling back across an area as part of a line of diggers. Everyone has their own pace but the line also has to move as a unit. What happens when the group is working well is that those who are moving quickly will adjust their speed by taking on a slightly broader front thus relieving the pressure on those who are working more slowly and so keeping the line together. An excavation is a co-operative enterprise not a competitive one (67). People who try to shift a heavier barrow than the next person are simply inflating their own egos and lining up for an accident.

As you are likely to be working next to a number of people for some length of time you will need to talk to them. This may seem obvious

65 Making observations of contemporary features can lead to new archaeological interpretations.

but there are both diggers who seem unable to chat and directors who try and stop it. Few people enjoy working next to someone who appears to be morose and incapable of passing the time of day but on the other hand a compulsive chatterer can be even harder to dig alongside. In practice talking about the job in hand is vital for passing on information and checking your own impressions of what is going on. If you are working in the kind of environment where there is a free exchange of comment you are far less likely to find yourself struggling as there will be a consensus about what has to be done. Digging does have its dull moments which can best be enlivened by conversation.

Those new to digging find it hard to pace themselves effectively. Two or three weeks of digging can impose great strains on one's physical and emotional well-being. Just as the athlete with a long race ahead will warm up and begin slowly, so the digger needs to break him or herself in gently and take things steadily. There is always a falling away amongst diggers as an excavation continues and many of those who cannot last the course have simply worked themselves too hard and become worn out.

The other main reason for diggers giving up is a sense of disillusionment with the progress the excavation seems to be making and their own lack of progress on to more interesting and important jobs. There

66 Cave houses near Kinver, Staffordshire, a photograph from the Stone Collection around 1900. All that survives today are some rough holes in the cliff face. (Reproduced by permission of Birmingham Library Services.)

67 Working together: mopping up after a downpour.

are excavations where it is a matter of policy to pass on to the excavators as much responsibility as possible for things such as recording. They tend to have a lower wastage rate than those digs where there is a sense that the newcomer has a kind of apprenticeship to serve which involves moving spoil heaps and other unattractive tasks. Everyone should be keen to advance their own expertise and every dig should make opportunities to promote 'in-service training'. In practice if you maintain a keen interest in the overall progress of the dig and show yourself willing to help and ready to learn then most directors and supervisors will recognize that interest and reward it.

5 Excavations – getting down to earth

The principles of excavation

In the past people went about the business of their daily lives, waking and sleeping, eating and drinking, creating and destroying. Each of these activities had some effect on the world around them. The impact on their environment varied from the imperceptible to the radical. Equally variable are the traces of the changes made which have survived to the present. Sometimes the ephemeral is preserved by accident as with a thumb print made in once wet plaster. Other events brought about such alterations that the environmental consequences are with us today. The excavator is interested in these events and their aftermath. Objects are important too but mainly, as we shall see, for the light they throw on what has been going on.

In outline the process of excavation is simple, in detail it becomes extraordinarily complex. The basic principle is that you begin with the most recent deposit and remove it. The next most recent material is then removed and so on moving back through time digging up the remains of human activity in reverse order until nothing remains but undisturbed 'natural'. Each deposit is recorded in as much detail as possible and the results analysed to produce a chronological narrative of events in which the sequence ancient to modern is restored (68).

On a practical level the first question facing the archaeologist on site is exactly how is a deposit defined? It is a question which has a lot to do with the way an excavator imposes his or her own sense of order on the jumble of earth, rock and rubbish that lies under our feet. Imagine working on a green field site. A 10 m square has been marked out and work is about to begin (69). Obviously the turf and the litter scattered about on it represent the contemporary scene but what next? Once the turf has been carefully cut and lifted and the loose dirt cleaned up what is revealed? There could be the remains of a buried stone wall, a dump of broken roof tiles, a spread of well-packed pebbles which

68 Excavations at Pouzay, France. A Roman temple uncovered in a 5 m square following the removal of the topsoil.

69 Plan of an imaginary site set out in a 10 m square.

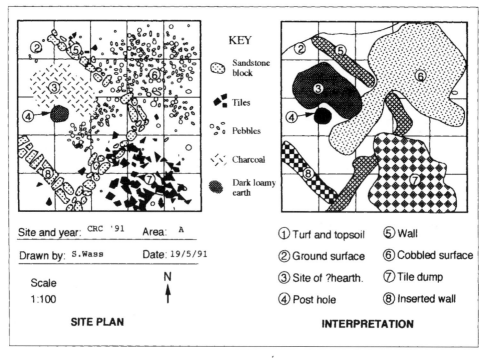

KEY

Sandstone block

Tiles

Pebbles

Charcoal

Dark loamy earth

Site and year: CRC '91   Area: A

Drawn by: S.Wass   Date: 19/5/91

Scale 1:100

N

SITE PLAN

① Turf and topsoil   ⑤ Wall
② Ground surface   ⑥ Cobbled surface
③ Site of ?hearth.   ⑦ Tile dump
④ Post hole   ⑧ Inserted wall

INTERPRETATION

might have been a cobbled yard, and several different coloured patches of soil. In the archaeologists' technical vocabulary each of these features is referred to as a **context**.

The dictionary will tell you that 'context' is a literary term referring to the setting of a word or phrase that clarifies its meaning. It has come into archaeological use through references to the 'context' in which a particular object may have been found but now it is used to label any archaeological deposit which can be defined as having an existence separate from the contexts around it. An alternative view, presented by the Central Excavation Unit in 1977, is that a context is 'the smallest entity, other than a removable object, about which useful data may be recorded'. Whatever the phraseology used an archaeological context is something created by an archaeologist to give meaning to a site (70).

Returning to our fictitious site some parts of the exposed area can readily be defined as contexts. The wall, the tile dump and the cobbles all stand out as being clearly different to their surroundings. The patches of soil may need more careful examination. Further cleaning may reveal a roughly circular patch of looser darker soil which may be the filling of a rubbish pit. Close by is a spread of charcoal and ash

70 Excavations at Repton, Derbyshire. Each separate context is marked with a white label.

113

which may mark the site of a fire. The two are both set in a layer of lighter coloured loamy clay which seems to extend over the whole of the rest of the area. Each of these can usefully be labelled a context.

A number of contexts grouped together are sometimes described as a **feature**, while a single context which extends across an area may be termed a **layer**. One of the hardest ideas to grasp is that a context can also be used to describe an absence of material as when a pit or ditch has been dug. Obviously the silting and other debris which fills these gaps may all be described as contexts but so too can the cut itself. More specifically these are **negative features** in which other contexts accumulate. There are also contexts or features, such as banks or walls, which stood proud of a surface and against which other contexts built up. These are **positive features**.

Once the uncovered contexts have been identified and labelled the archaeologist is then faced with the task of recording as much useful information as possible about the features exposed in the 10 m square. At some point in the future it might be possible to recognize and record every scrap of information available on site down to the position and chemical composition of the last grain of sand. We are some way from this point and in practice have to be extremely selective about what we record. This selectivity is governed both by our own perceptions, most notably what we see in front of us expressed in terms of texture and colour, and by the amount of information we can usefully handle and store.

Perceptiveness is a great benefit to an excavator but it can also be something of a handicap. Many of the patterns left behind by human activity are so slight and the indications so subtle that nothing but the human eye could ever pick them out. During excavations of the later phases of the Roman town at Wroxeter small differences in the patterns of wear on cobbled surfaces provided clues about a whole series of hitherto unsuspected timber buildings. Unfortunately the brain's ability to recognize patterns is balanced by a tendency to identify patterns where no patterns exist. Most excavators have had the experience of plotting random spreads of pebbles to create cobbled yards or investing scatters of post-holes with the kind of order that produces villages of round huts, or were they square?

The other factor which influences the information collected is the kind of interpretations that are made of the different features as they are exposed. There is an expectation that the excavator should be detached from the process of digging, operating in a way which is both objective and impartial. In practice it would be impossible to dig intelligently without a continual process of interpretation and then reinterpretation going on. Many diggers will keep up an internal mono-logue which goes something like this: 'Ah, now, there is a stone here, and another one...this looks like the beginning of a wall...here's another stone, seems a bit loose though. And down this side? Hm...yes, a few pebbles...they seem well set in...a cobbled yard perhaps...or a floor? So what's on the other side? Quite a few tiles here...slipped from the roof...some seem burnt, perhaps there was a fire and the roof collapsed...' These kinds of question and answer are the first steps towards understanding a site. Their importance is underlined by the fact that as the excavator you may be the sole individual able to make pronouncements about the material you have been working on.

Returning to our theoretical 10 m square things have been going very smoothly. A number of contexts have been identified and described and the site seems to be making sense as some sort of story unfolds. As we take things apart we are able to assign to them their place in the story by virtue of their relationship with each other. The key to this is the principle of **stratigraphy**. In the nineteenth century geologists studying the earth's structure discovered that generally speaking, where a series of rocks had been laid down in horizontal bands the older rocks were at the bottom and the newer ones at the top. This notion of stratification has become an important interpretative tool for the archaeologist. One that again is simple in principle but can become complicated in reality (71).

On our specimen site the dump of tiles overlays the wall and must therefore be more recent. The cobbled surface is partially covered by the charcoal and so must be earlier. The cobbles are laid against the wall and so are later. This is sometimes expressed as the wall being **primary** to the cobbles or the cobbles being **secondary** to the wall. This is an example of a **relative chronology** with the wall pre-dating the cobbles which pre-date the charcoal. The relationship between the tiles and the charcoal remains uncertain. This sequence is floating free in time and we need something to anchor it to a specific period. Finds now become important. Within each context there are likely to be a number of recognizable fragments of objects left by human activity on the site. These can range from pottery to metalwork which, as well as providing information on the kinds of activities undertaken, can also help date it. One might expect that the very best evidence that one could have would be a coin, after all an actual date may well be stamped on its face, but there are complications.

The first problem is that small objects can move about in the soil long after they have been buried. This happens both naturally through a combination of the effects of burrowing animals and the tug of gravity

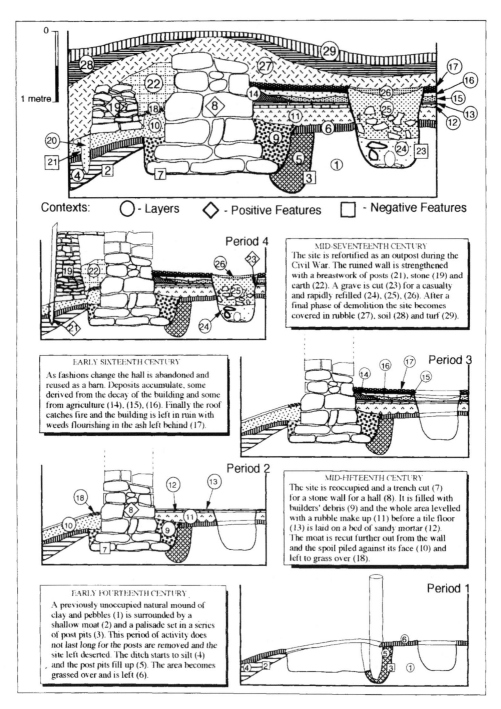

Contexts: ◯ - Layers   ◇ - Positive Features   ▢ - Negative Features

Period 4

MID-SEVENTEENTH CENTURY

The site is refortified as an outpost during the Civil War. The ruined wall is strengthened with a breastwork of posts (21), stone (19) and earth (22). A grave is cut (23) for a casualty and rapidly refilled (24), (25), (26). After a final phase of demolition the site becomes covered in rubble (27), soil (28) and turf (29).

EARLY SIXTEENTH CENTURY

As fashions change the hall is abandoned and reused as a barn. Deposits accumulate, some derived from the decay of the building and some from agriculture (14), (15), (16). Finally the roof catches fire and the building is left in ruin with weeds flourishing in the ash left behind (17).

Period 3

Period 2

MID-FIFTEENTH CENTURY

The site is reoccupied and a trench cut (7) for a stone wall for a hall (8). It is filled with builders' debris (9) and the whole area levelled with a rubble make up (11) before a tile floor (13) is laid on a bed of sandy mortar (12). The moat is recut further out from the wall and the spoil piled against its face (10) and left to grass over (18).

EARLY FOURTEENTH CENTURY

A previously unoccupied natural mound of clay and pebbles (1) is surrounded by a shallow moat (2) and a palisade set in a series of post pits (3). This period of activity does not last long for the posts are removed and the site left deserted. The ditch starts to silt (4) and the post pits fill up (5). The area becomes grassed over and is left (6).

Period 1

116

and less naturally as a result of human disturbance. This means that they are no longer associated with the context on to which they were dropped. Difficulties with dating continue, for even if they are securely linked to a particular feature, perhaps mortared into a wall, they can only tell us the date after which they were deposited. Valuable or attractive objects may well be treasured for centuries before being lost. The wall with a Roman coin of the first century AD built into its foundations cannot be earlier than this date but it could belong to any period after it.

Pottery and other manufactured items which are cheap and/or fragile can often offer more useful guidance for dating. Study of changes in the materials and the ways they have been used, both from a technological and stylistic point of view, provide a sequence for dating everyday items relatively. These sequences can then be linked to a chronological framework through work on similar sites where the archaeological remains are firmly associated with a known historical event. Burnt articles found during excavations in London may be related either to the burning of Londinium in AD 61 following the revolt of Queen Boudica or to the Great Fire of 1666, depending, of course, on the contexts within which they are found. Usually a large collection of short-lived objects is more helpful for dating than the occasional find of one or two precious items. There are, of course, several other scientific dating methods based on the physical and chemical analysis of remains.

The archaeologists have made an initial assessment of the dating evidence available on our fictional site. The tiles in the dump, context 7, are clearly Roman and there is Roman pottery in the charcoal spread, context 3, which overlays the cobbled floor. This is obviously a Roman building. It is decided to take off context 7, the dump of roof tiles, as the next most recent deposit and suddenly things are no longer quite so straightforward stratigraphically. Our site is actually on a terrace on a hillside and it becomes clear that the tiles have slipped down from a point further up the hill, outside the excavated area. Further work reveals that the charcoal spread is actually the upcast from digging a large pit, context 4. What seemed to be established fact is now a theory which looks increasingly shaky. Even the size and shape of the building are called into question when it is discovered that erosion on the downhill side of the terrace has removed the corner of the building. So work continues, further questions are answered or shelved as the evidence is removed and recorded. By the end of the season, through the application of hard work, some talent, considerable expertise, a pinch of inspiration and not a little luck a convincing story emerges.

71 Stratigraphy, interpreting a section through an imaginary medieval site.

Tools of the trade

On first starting work the most common task the beginner is likely to be given is trowelling. This will probably involve scraping across a more or less flat area to expose a new surface for study. The supervisor will ask for the area to be 'taken down' or 'cleaned up' and trowels will be given out. No ordinary garden centre tools these, but 10 cm (4 in) pointing trowels (72). They are available from good hardware stores and builders' merchants. Most diggers purchase one at an early stage in their careers and become very possessive about them. If you do buy your own, the first thing to do is mark it with your initials either by carving or branding them into the wooden handle, anything else will eventually wear off! This particular tool is specified because the size and shape of the blade are correct for the kind of jobs you will be asked to do and also because the blade and handle are forged from a single piece of steel so there are no rivets to come undone. Some old hands prefer to have a couple of trowels at their side. One will be worn or cut down to about 4 or 5 cm (2 in) for use on hard ground or for precise working while the other will be full size for shifting looser material more quickly. Several other fine tools can be employed for more delicate work ranging from palette knives and teaspoons to dental probes and tooth picks. Most diggers will gradually build up their own tool kit which will reflect their special interests.

72 Solid forged pointing trowels, in two sizes.

In skilled hands the trowel can become either a precise implement for working on fragile materials or a powerful tool for removing large quantities of spoil. It is normally used on edge and pulled in towards the kneeling excavator with a scraping motion. This removes a couple of millimetres or so of the surface being worked on. The fresh exposed surface will show the colours and textures typical of the context being removed or else something will have changed and you will be through to the next context down. Sometimes the point is used to loosen the soil but care has to be taken not to dig holes that may penetrate down through underlying layers.

It is important while trowelling not to let too much loose earth accumulate. By your side you will have a small hand shovel and a bucket. Once there is enough soil to fill the shovel it is scraped up and transferred to the bucket, once the bucket is full it is transferred to the wheelbarrow and once the wheelbarrow is full it is emptied on to the spoil heap. If a lot of spoil is left lying about not only will it obscure the surface you are working on it also makes life difficult if you are trying to track down the origin of a small find you suddenly discover lying loose by the point of your trowel!

If a large area is to be cleared by trowelling you will probably find yourself part of a line which is moving slowly but steadily backwards (73). From a kneeling or squatting position you will clean the ground in front of you. The position is not a particularly comfortable one and some people use kneeling mats or knee pads to alleviate the pain. Nevertheless it is important to work this way so that you always have an expanse of freshly exposed ground in front of you to pick up any changes to the context as they occur. It will also ensure that you do not mark the cleaned surface by shuffling across it as you dig.

When trowelling in this way the chief difficulty lies in knowing how much to remove, or, more accurately, when to stop. If the job is simply one of cleaning an already excavated surface then the aim is simple, to remove as little as possible while clearing the site of any loose particles which will have dried out and so obscured the colours and textures before you. If you have an old context to remove, the chances are that nobody knows exactly what lies underneath. Instructions like, 'Dig down until you hit red clay', or 'Remove this down to the pebble surface' are likely to prove disastrous. As you are moving into the unknown a better piece of advice would be, 'Remove this carefully until you come to something different and then stop'. The appearance of a newly cleaned surface should be allowed to 'speak for itself'. This means that the excavator should not introduce new and potentially misleading marks, colours or textures as a result of their trowelling

73 A line of
trowellers working
across the centre of a
large barrow at
Guiting Power.

technique, instead the digger will need to learn to finish off with an exceptionally light touch.

As well as using the edge to scrape, the point of the trowel can be used with care, sometimes gently, perhaps to tease out a few loose particles of dirt from around a bone and sometimes strongly with a downwards chopping motion on thick and compacted materials. Whatever the methods used most of the effort in using a trowel comes from the shoulders and most of the stress occurs in the wrist. As with any repetitive movement it is best to work rhythmically and with the minimum effort needed to make progress. This might mean peeling off a couple of millimetres from the surface and then going back for a second pass rather than trying to pull up large chunks at a time which is, of course, bad archaeology anyway. Experienced diggers sometimes cultivate the ability to dig either right- or left-handed so that the work load is spread more evenly.

On dry surfaces a brush can be extremely useful for removing dust and other small particles of dirt. With something like a cobbled floor a brush can save a lot of work taking loose out from amongst the pebbles, and on buried masonry its use can be essential to avoid marking soft stone with the trowel. A variety of brushes with different strengths of bristle and in different sizes should be available. In general the harder and drier the ground the more severe a brushing it will take.

120

However, there comes a point with very fine dust when only a soft brush will do the job. Unfortunately the slightest trace of moisture renders a brush quite unusable, for rather than clearing the dirt away it gets smeared across the surface obscuring the colour and the bristles dig in destroying the texture. People get shouted at for using brushes when it is wet.

Although much of an excavator's time will be spent removing earth in teaspoon-size quantities there will also be a need to dig out large amounts of spoil. Many sites use light mechanical excavators for this work but there will always be occasions when their use will be inappropriate or unsafe and human muscle power has to take over. There was a time when canals were dug and railway embankments built by gangs of navvies working with pick and shovel. Until quite recently they could still be seen at work mending the roads, but now even small trenches for pipes are cut by mini-excavators. The day of the hand tool is all but past except on archaeological digs. An excavation is one of the few places in Britain where labourers can still be seen wielding pick and shovel. In the early days of excavation it was normal to employ teams of professional navvies who really knew their tools and the best way to use them effectively and safely. Much of this expertise has been lost and it is all too common now to see volunteers turned loose with a pickaxe and no very clear idea what to do with it.

Hand tools such as the pick, mattock and fork are used to loosen the earth while a shovel is the best implement for shifting quantities of spoil. As with most tools the key to success is being well balanced and using the weight of the tool to work for you. When it comes to removing spoil from the site it is important to be able to judge the size of a load and know the kinds of amount that you can shift in comfort. If you are working well under your capacity you will be wasting time and effort making additional trips with your bucket or barrow, on the other hand if you try to lift too much you will rapidly tire and an accident may result. There will always be people who at the start of an excavation set out to prove that they can move more spoil than anyone else and so they labour with overflowing buckets and totter off with overloaded barrows; they rarely last long.

The best buckets to use are those with strong black plastic bodies and substantial wire and wood handles as sold to the building trade. Any kind of plastic household bucket will fall apart within hours. On some sites you may find all metal buckets in use but they are very heavy and can be a danger if dropped even when empty. A key principle in removing spoil is not to carry the same dirt around with you. This can be avoided by scraping the bottom of the bucket out each time you empty it, particularly if the material is wet. In damp weather it is also worth periodically checking the underneath of the bucket to remove any mud which may have gathered there. Buckets can be in short supply on a dig where a lot of trowelling is being done, even so, it is generally better to work with two whenever possible. It is easier, safer and more productive to move two three-quarter full buckets than one full one. Once more this is a question of balance. A single heavy bucket will drag against the legs and have to be counterbalanced by extravagant wavings of the other arm, two buckets balance each other.

The same requirements apply to wheelbarrows. When loading a barrow it is important to keep as much of the weight as possible towards the front end, over the axle, and to ensure that it is not unbalanced to one side or the other. Again it is important to know your own strength and not overreach yourself. Wet soil makes for heavier loads, as do fine sandy materials which pack down more than normal soil. Loads of rubble need watching not only because of their weight but because they can sometimes shift alarmingly in transit.

Once you are ready to go, grip the handles securely and lean into the load as you lift it to get maximum forward movement. Once you have overcome the initial inertia the secret is not to stop. In this respect it is a bit like riding a bicycle in terms of balance and pushing a car in terms of keeping up the momentum. To this end it is important that any route used by barrows is kept clear. Despite better alternatives being available in the way of tracking, many digs still rely on scaffolding planks to build their barrow runs. You owe it to yourself always to check a barrow run carefully before using it. If you have any doubts at all as to its safety only take half loads or indeed ask someone to sort it out. The gradients should never be too steep and the planks securely bedded and free from dirt. In rainy weather planks become quite impossible, you should never attempt to take a full barrow up a wet plank. If you are tipping out on to a spoil heap then no great finesse is required but filling skips from planks is a different matter. All barrows have a metal 'nose' in front of the wheel on which the barrow can be stood to empty it. If you are attempting this from the end of a plank you will need to judge things carefully so that the nose balances without slipping off into the skip. If you feel a barrow beginning to tip it is better to let it go and get out of the way rather than risk a serious sprain trying to wrestle it upright again.

Earthmoving machinery and other items of heavy plant have been a common feature of excavations, especially urban ones, for many years. They tend to be operated by professional drivers and all the average volunteer has to do is keep out of their way. However, much lighter pieces of equipment are now available on a self-drive basis and are becoming widely used. The kind of vehicle that can be hired by the day or week is usually on caterpillar tracks with a small bulldozer blade at one end and a bucket on the end of a hydraulic arm at the other. They can be very useful in relieving the digging team of many hours of labour. However, great care needs to be taken by anyone trundling round a busy archaeological site with such a machine. As far as the volunteer is concerned it is important to give these machines as wide a berth as possible, making allowances for the fact that the operator is almost certainly going to be inexperienced. People working nearby should wear safety helmets and no one should work in close proximity to such a machine until it has been switched off and the arm lowered to the ground.

On most sites the end of the working session is heralded by the cry, 'Clear up your loose!' It is normal practice at break times and the end of the day to remove all spoil from the site, gather the tools together and, if rain is threatened, cover them with an upturned bucket or barrow. This does away with the need for a break-neck rush back on to site to clear up should it start raining. At the very end of the day all tools, buckets and barrows will need cleaning before being put away. In dry conditions this may be little more than a brush down but if the tools are muddy they will have to be washed. If this is not done the mud will dry and can set as hard as concrete. Sometimes in very dry conditions the wooden handles of tools can shrink and work loose; in these circumstances an overnight soak in a bucket of water should tighten them up again. As a volunteer you have, in common with everyone else, a duty to care for the tools; a good set can make the difference between a safe and productive site and a dangerous and frustrating one.

Site organization

Because all excavation is based on team work it is important that good communications are at the centre of any management structure. People need to know who is responsible for what and to whom they are answerable and exactly what is going on. Most excavations operate a chain of command which begins with the director. Although accountable to whoever is paying the bills, he or she will actually have overall responsibility for managing the project and will normally see it through from planning to completion. Under the director are the site supervisors who are each responsible for the day-to-day supervision of a particular area or task. Also amongst the ranks of 'middle management' will be found individuals with responsibility for activities such as surveying, finds processing and other specialist jobs. Then there are the diggers who will be divided on a fairly flexible basis between the various supervisory staff. The site supervisors report to the director on what progress has been made, and following discussion will then take general instructions, to which they will add detail, and pass them on to the work-force. The amount of contact between the ordinary volunteer and the senior management can vary depending on the scale of the dig and the temperament of the director. Some are distant figures glimpsed only occasionally while others make it their business to dig alongside everyone else on a regular basis.

The daily timetable within which all this takes place can be a demanding one. Work will normally begin at 9.00 am. The morning session may well take 15 or 20 minutes to get underway as tools and tasks are given out. A 15-minute coffee break around 11.00 am is followed by an hour's lunch break at 1.00 pm. An afternoon tea break will be at 4.00 pm, with knocking off time normally at 6.00 or 6.30 pm. This is an eight-hour working day, six days a week. While the hours can seem long, generally the work has its own fascination and the time slips away quite rapidly. When the job does become wearing then it is time to ask for a change! In practice good management should ensure that both the needs of the project and the individuals contributing to it are continually being assessed and adjustments made to the routine.

74 Work in progress on the industrial site.

124

On a busy site the picture can resemble a disturbed ants' nest (**74**). However, all the activity is purposeful and gradually, after a few minutes, the watching eye should discern a pattern emerging from the chaos. The scene will focus on the ground under excavation, normally a rectangular area based on a 2 m grid. It will probably be surrounded by white wooden pegs set back a metre or two from the edge of the trench and marking the boundaries of the grid. The sides of the area, referred to as the **section edge**, are likely to be given special care and attention as they offer a vertical view down through the site as excavated to date. There may be a variety of lines criss-crossing the site, some, carefully levelled, will be used to draw additional sections through the excavated surfaces, while others will be there to help with the labelling of finds or drawing of plans. Sometimes strips of ground or **baulks** will be left undug, either to offer access to parts of the site or to provide sections that can be drawn prior to the baulk's eventual removal. The whole area will probably be fenced in to include a tool shed and a site hut. This latter, which these days is often one of the range of portable buildings, takes on the job of a site office, a canteen and a shelter from the rain (**75**).

The most obvious activity, and the one which tends to define most patterns of movement, is the removal of spoil. After all excavation is really just the digging of a very large hole and the waste material from that hole has to be got rid of. On some large sites the spoil is taken away on conveyor belts and dumped into skips but if the excavation

75 Sometimes it is necessary to do a little improvising. Site 'hut' at Pouzay, France.

is likely to be back-filled then it may well be kept close at hand.

Most people on site will be digging with a variety of tools in a variety of ways, picks and shovels and mechanical excavators may be being used if a lot of overburden has to be shifted, but normally people will be on their hands and knees digging with a trowel. Depending on the stage of the excavation, they may be working together in a line to strip a whole area or else dispersed in small groups examining particular features. Other individuals will probably be busy writing, drawing or taking photographs as part of the recording process. There is a tendency for sites to begin simply and then break up into smaller complex units scattered here and there and each at different stages of excavation. The whole site can end up as a potential minefield to the unwary with the most common question heard being 'Is it safe to walk here?'

Making sense of it all

Although each site is unique there are a series of common features which turn up more or less regularly and which present their own problems, both in terms of stratigraphy and digging.

Post-holes and pits

It is impossible to dig a hole in the ground and fill it in again without that disturbance becoming part of the archaeological record. Holes are dug for three main reasons: for building; for storage; and to dispose of rubbish. Just as today we will put up posts to support our garden fence, so, in the past, entire buildings were erected based on earthfast posts. Some were minor structures but one of the Saxon palaces excavated at Yeavering was 30 m (98 ft) long by 9 m (30 ft) wide. As an alternative to digging individual sockets for single posts a trench would be cut to accommodate lines of posts. Once in place they would often be packed round with rubble to hold them secure before the hole was back-filled. The appearance of a post-hole in the ground rather depends on the fate of the building. If it was left to fall apart naturally the base of the post may well appear as a darker circle within the disturbed fill of the post-hole. If the structure was taken apart the post may have been wrenched out of the ground or else the whole pit could have been dug out to recover the post intact. Because of the speed at which many wooden posts decayed in the ground, timber buildings were frequently rebuilt either in the same place or on a slightly different alignment. This can lead to a confusing situation on the ground and considerable time may have to be spent disentangling the different phases of building.

As an alternative to digging post-holes and continually having to renovate rotten timbers some structures had their vertical posts set on large flat stones called pad-stones. It is sometimes possible to see a sequence of several generations of post-holes eventually replaced by pad-stones.

During excavation post-holes are emptied to clarify the plan of the structure and recover information as to how it was built. A post-hole will normally appear as a roughly circular patch of soil slightly darker than the surroundings and perhaps looser in texture. The first step is carefully to clean the entire area to determine its size and shape. This will probably be drawn. If you were proceeding according to strict stratigraphic principles you would then define and remove the remains of the post itself before removing the rest of the back-fill plus any packing. In practice some people will put a line across the top and empty out half of the post-hole so that they can see and draw the filling in section before removing the other half (76).

In prehistoric times pits were used to store cereals and then often converted into rubbish dumps. In later periods pits were dug almost

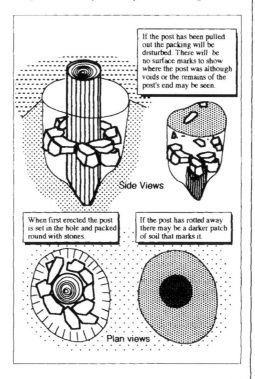

76 Post-holes.

If the post has been pulled out the packing will be disturbed. There will be no surface marks to show where the post was although voids or the remains of the post's end may be seen.

Side Views

When first erected the post is set in the hole and packed round with stones.

If the post has rotted away there may be a darker patch of soil that marks it.

Plan views

exclusively for this purpose. Some of the most rewarding of these are cess pits of medieval and later times. Few people would bother to clamber down into their cess pit to recover lost possessions so there they stayed. Large pits may contain many layers of fill and even contain smaller structures within them. Again it is common practice to remove the contents so that the sections, perhaps along and across the pit, can be drawn.

Walls

The walls of wooden buildings do not normally show up well during excavation. They may have been simply of wattle and daub, a combination of mud, dung and straw plastered on to a woven wooden frame which only tends to survive if it has been burnt. Sometimes a horizontal wooden beam called a sleeper or sill beam would be laid on the ground as a foundation for a timber frame or wooden panelling. If these have been left to decay *in situ* they will appear as a shallow straight-sided gully with a darker fill. These are sometimes known as timber slots. Low walls of stone are found occasionally, with little in the way of foundations. They were used to lift the sleeper beam off the damp earth and so prolong its life and are called sleeper walls (77).

Masonry walls are almost always trench built. A foundation or construction trench would be dug, sometimes cutting through earlier layers. Foundations would be laid, the wall built and then the trench filled in, usually with the builder's rubbish that was lying around. Major walls would have two outer faces built perhaps of dressed stone sandwiching a core of loose rubble, mortar, plaster and mud. In places

77 Methods of wall construction.

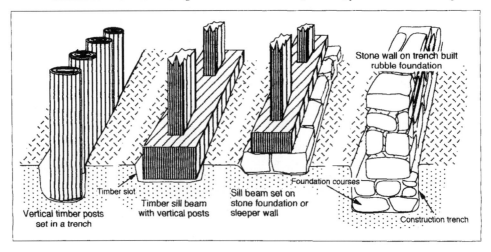

Stone wall on trench built rubble foundation

Foundation courses

Timber slot

Timber sill beam with vertical posts

Sill beam set on stone foundation or sleeper wall

Vertical timber posts set in a trench

Construction trench

where building stone was at a premium the remains of the walls of a derelict building would be robbed, sometimes to the point of actually digging out the foundations by means of a robber trench. There are many major stone buildings which are only known as ghosts of their former selves through the excavation of robbing trenches (78).

78 Partially robbed out remains of the wall of the north aisle, Bordesley Abbey.

Floors

A range of materials was used in the past to provide surfaces on which to live and work. The most common of these, even in quite grand buildings, was dirt. Dirt or earth floors can be surprisingly easy to recognize. The combination of the compacting effect of the floor's construction and use together with the darkening effect of the rubbish trodden into it produces a solid layer of near black, laminated, silty material. A natural alternative for a harder wearing surface, especially outside, is a cobbled floor. Pebbles are readily available in most areas of the country and when set in clay provide a substantial if somewhat uncomfortable surface to walk on. In both Roman and medieval times floors of mortar, plaster, stone and tile were laid and if intact make for easy digging. A number of floors have been encountered where tiles

129

79 Excavating floor levels with the remains of tile impressions on a mortar surface.

have been lifted and the only evidence of their passing is the impressions they have left in the mortar bedding (79).

Of course any floor surface will be subject to erosion and once wear sets in the users have two choices. One is to scrap the whole thing and lay a new floor over the top and the other is to repair it. There may be a series of floor levels superimposed on each other, building up a depth of stratification which may amount to a metre or more. Frequently the ground is prepared for a new floor by levelling it up with a spread of 'make up' which may consist of clay, rubble or sand. Repairs using similar materials often meant that holes would be patched with a couple of buckets full of whatever came to hand trodden into the surface. The best place to study the patchwork effect this created is in any modern car park. The principle of only taking off a single context at a time without digging holes becomes particularly important on a floor where there may be several thin interleaving layers of construction and repair.

130

Ditches

Ditches have been cut and maintained for a variety of purposes: for drainage or for the supply of water; to mark boundaries; and as defensive barriers. The main problem with a ditch is that as soon as it has been dug out it starts to fill back up again with silt, organic debris and rubbish. The way this happens depends on what materials the ditch has been cut through, how the banks were constructed and whether the ditch is dry or wet, with flowing or standing water. A section cut through a naturally silted ditch will tend to show several layers of material reflecting changes in conditions. Of course a ditch can be filled in on purpose if it is no longer needed, or cleaned out to keep it functioning. A ditch may simply be scoured out, which has no overall effect on its original profile, but does remove all the accumulated silts. Alternatively it may be completely recut, perhaps on a slightly different alignment and possibly several times in succession.

This pattern of erosion, deposition and recutting can make lengths of ditch amongst the hardest features to excavate successfully. There was a time when most ditches were simply sectioned with a trench cut across them at right angles. Today ditches are more likely to be completely excavated as part of a wider open area. This is important

80 Section across an imaginary prehistoric ditch and bank showing silting and recuts.

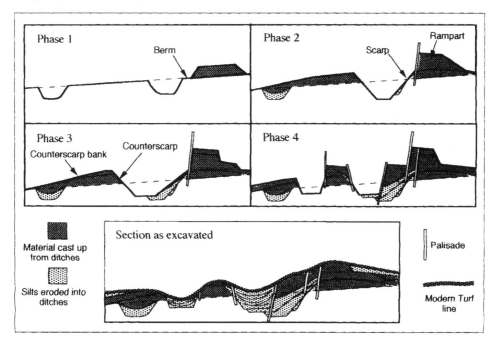

131

because it has been shown how radically the nature of a feature such as a ditch can change in just a few metres. It also helps in gaining information about associated features such as palisades, linings and sluices (80).

Banks

Banks or ramparts tend to complement ditches, being formed from the material thrown out from them, and as such they perform many of the same functions. Just as a ditch starts to fill up so a bank will start to slip away and its appearance in an excavation may be much reduced. Most banks were actually constructed with some care and may feature retaining walls of stone or timber and internal tip lines where layers of different materials were dumped and spread. Many banks were crowned with a fence or palisade and so the tops need careful examination for evidence of lines of post-holes. An added bonus with banks is that they will seal below them the buried ground surface on which they were built. This gives us the opportunity to examine conditions on site before building began. Sections are still important aids to understanding how a bank has been put together but again they are increasingly being dug at length and in detail.

Waterlogged wood

As the technology has developed to cope with the conditions and preserve the finds much work has been done on wetland sites. Damp conditions can preserve wood in a way which can seem almost miraculous. It is not the water that acts as a preservative but the fact that in waterlogged conditions any oxygen in the ground is soon used up and so the bacteria and fungi which would have attacked the wood cannot survive. Work on these sites will feature elaborate arrangements for keeping the water level at just the right point: not enough and the site dries out, too much and the diggers drown. Attention has to be paid to questions of access to the site. Although well preserved, waterlogged materials are frequently extremely fragile and may have to be worked on from some kind of suspended platform. Most wetland sites are a tangle of soggy wood and clinging silts needing sensitive excavation and detailed recording.

Graves

Graves (81) are a special case in excavation for a number of reasons. The most obvious of these is that the handling of human remains requires a sensitive, some might say reverent approach. The work is not to everyone's liking and nobody should be asked to dig a grave if it causes

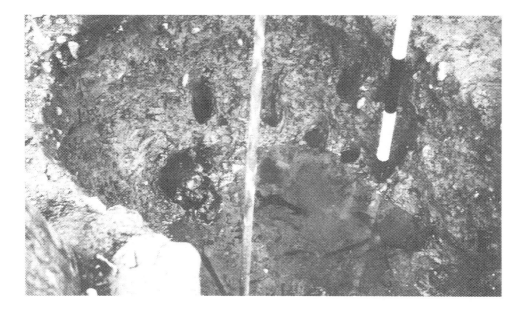

them distress. To do the job well demands an unusually high standard of excavation particularly in the recovery of skeletal and other remains.

The actual process is quite simple, firstly the edge of the cut for the grave will have to be defined. A grave is like any other hole except for the fact that as the fill may have been shovelled back within a matter of hours of having been dug out the changes are not always easy to detect. Work will then begin on removing the fill carefully, watching for surviving remains of a coffin. This will usually be either in the form of staining, where the timber has rotted, or metal fragments of nails or the coffin's fittings. It is usually known which way the grave is oriented and so where the head is likely to be. Some diggers, as they scrape away the fill, will begin each pass at the head end. As the skull generally is the highest part of the skeleton and one of the most robust, identifying its position at an early stage makes the rest of the job a little easier. The final cleaning of the skeleton itself requires hours of delicate work.

Burials often occur in large numbers and excavations working with them will have their own record-keeping system to streamline the recording of the skeleton. Bones will normally be lifted and removed for further study. Examination of skeletal remains, especially in large quantities, can provide valuable information about the general health and composition of a population. In normal practice the police are

81 An excavated grave. The stake holes are not an attempt to pin down a vampire but result from work on the foundations of the south-east corner of the south transept at Bordesley Abbey.

informed whenever human remains are unearthed and photographs of burials inevitably find their way on to the front pages of the local papers. There is no doubt about the fascination graves hold for most of us and anyone digging one during an open day will have to be prepared for a large audience.

Ephemera

Every now and then something turns up which through some chance set of circumstances has been preserved against all the odds and suddenly one feels in touch with the past. Here are three examples from the floor of the abbey church at Bordesley. When we came to investigate the surface on which builders of the twelfth-century church had worked we found that some patches of lime had been pressed down into the underlying clay. Their crescentic shape made us realize that we were probably looking at the hoof prints of pack horses which had been led in carrying supplies for the workmen. Secondly, we had suspected that the dirt floors which covered much of the early church were strewn with rushes but could find no evidence until a small carbonized fragment turned up, which under the magnifying glass showed the typical striations of a rush leaf. We conjectured that it may have been preserved there when a spark from a guttering candle fell to the ground and burned it. Finally when removing a dump of make-up from below a later floor we saw impressed on the dirt floor below a series of shallow ruts. Gradually a pattern emerged and we saw the tracks made by the wheelbarrows which had been trundled into the church with their loads of rubble. Every site has its record of chance finds and precious survivals but they only come to light as a result of careful excavation and good observation.

6 Excavations – the support services

Recording

An excavation is also served by a range of other people, apart from diggers, who support the work out on site in a variety of important ways. Some of the jobs they do are specialist ones which demand a high level of training, but others can be passed on to site supervisors and ordinary volunteers. The most important of these is the on-site recording of contexts. Policy on this can vary but many directors now believe that the best person to describe a context is the one who has just dug it. Digging certainly becomes more thoughtful and thorough when the prospect of having to fill out a record card begins to loom.

In the early years of excavation the main aids to recording were the site supervisors' and director's notebooks. Experience showed that recording in this way was often patchy, generally highly subjective and frequently impossible for anyone else to decipher. These days standardized recording forms of one kind or another are almost universal and bring with them a number of benefits. The main advantage of a common format is that it makes it much easier to share the work of recording between several people, giving them a common vocabulary for both discussing and reporting on the site. It is also a necessary precursor to capturing data by computer. The chief requirements of any recording system are that it is both easy to learn and easy to administer and that at a later date it is easy to extract the necessary information from it.

To begin with a decision has to be taken that a context can be identified and labelled. This will normally be made by the supervisor who will note its presence and number in a notebook kept for the purpose before writing out a label. These are usually written in waterproof ink on white plastic rectangles which are then pinned to the ground using a galvanized roofing nail.

Generally each context will be given a combination of letters and

82 Filling in context record cards.

numerals which are unique for the site and which will help locate it at a later date. For example CRC '89 A 026 refers to a site at Chapel Row Cropredy dug in 1989. The 'A' designation is a sub-division of the site locating the context inside the shell of a seventeenth-century cottage while the number 026 indicates that it was the twenty-sixth context to be numbered on this part of the site. Other excavations simply have a single set of numbers for use right across all areas, thus doing away with the need for further sub-divisions.

The best time to record a context is probably about two-thirds of the way through its excavation. Sufficient needs to have been dug for the excavator to have a good idea as to what is going on, but enough left so that any doubtful points that arise during the recording can be checked. It is best to fill in the record form on site, although in wet conditions it is normal to make a rough copy which can later be transferred to the final card (82). While the precise format will vary most standard record cards will include these features:

Site and year
This information should be written out in full. On large sites it is often over-printed on to all records.

Area code
If used this will normally be a letter although a few sites favour Roman numerals.

Context number

These are usually handed out sequentially, this will then reflect the order in which the contexts were identified and will not necessarily bear any relationship to their chronological order. It is not unusual for a large site to have over a thousand separate contexts numbered during the course of an excavation.

Description

A general description creates a setting for the information that follows and allows anyone leafing through the records a quick check on the kind of feature it is. The recorder may have considerable freedom of choice in selecting an appropriate form of words here although there is an obligation to be as objective and concise as possible. A 'shallow, oval clay-filled depression' would probably do while a 'muddy hole' would not. Descriptions such as 'a broad vertically-sided timber-lined gully' or 'a spread of burnt clay, charcoal and ash' both contain sufficient detail for the reader to picture the particular context.

How defined

It is important for evaluating the strength of the evidence later on to give some indication of how the context was revealed. A 'how defined' box enables the recorder to note whether the context was uncovered by careful trowelling or if it emerged as a smear in the side of a trench cut by a mechanical excavator.

Interpretation

As we have already noted archaeologists will re-interpret the contexts they are excavating and any written pronouncement is almost certain to be provisional. Nevertheless a time comes when the best possible guess, at the current stage of the dig, has to be written down. The broad vertically-sided timber-lined gully is probably a drain and the spread of burnt clay, charcoal and ash almost certainly a hearth and both will be noted as such. If nothing else, making a provisional identification of a post-hole or timber slot gives everyone a kind of verbal shorthand when discussing the site. 'The post-hole by your left foot' is much more manageable than 'PRM '91 E 462'.

Position

The location of a context can be defined in a variety of ways depending on the site and the character of the context. The whole area may have been divided up by a 1 or 2 m grid and each square given its own letter code. Alternatively a system of co-ordinates or grid references pinpointed on the approximate centre of the feature may be used. The point is to give the eventual user as accurate an idea as possible of just where on the site the context was located. More precise details of position will be taken down during the survey work which will follow.

Length, width/extent

These options ask for more precise details of size as measured with a hand-tape, sometimes 'diameter' may be included as an option for circular features. Dimensions are given conventionally in metres although centimetres may be used. Confusion can arise if the correct conventions are not observed:

2.46 metres (m)	=	246 centimetres (cm)
1.00 m	=	100 cm
0.74 m	=	74 cm
0.02 m	=	2 cm

Thickness/height/depth

These kinds of entries ask for measurement to be extended into the third dimension. It is sometimes only possible to complete this section after the whole context has been removed, as with the filling of a pit.

Levels

Sometimes it is helpful to have a record of the level of the upper surface of the context as it relates to the site datum. This can be measured with an optical level and staff (see Chapter 2). If the context is sloping then levels can be given on to different spots, for example:

E end −0.78 m b.s.d., W end −0.88 m b.s.d. (b.s.d.: below site datum)

Composition

This section enables the excavator to record in detail the nature of the deposit. Under this heading should be listed the chief components of the context together with some idea of relative percentages. Typical entries might read, 'Clean sandy loam (70%) with small- to medium-sized pebbles (25%) with fragments of broken tile (5%)', or 'Thick blackish silt (60%) with spreads of organic debris (30%) and occasional patches of brown sand (10%)'.

Colour

Colour is an important descriptive feature but both colour names and the actual perception of colour itself can vary enormously. To overcome

83 Using a Munsell Colour Chart.

this problem many people refer to a set of standard colour charts prepared expressly for soil analysis. These are known as the 'Munsell Soil Colour Charts' named after their American compiler (83). Sample colours are grouped according to three variables. These are **hue** which relates to the colour's position on the spectrum, **value** which is a measure of the lightness or darkness of the colour and **chroma** which describes its purity. The soil that is being described has to be slightly moist and the surface freshly exposed. Once a good match has been found the colour can then be noted both with a standard name and in figures, for example 'Dark Yellowish Brown 10YR 4/4'.

Texture

Specialist terminology is once more needed to describe those properties which relate to the size of particles present in the soil. Four standard terms tend to be used. **Sand** describes particles between 2 and 0.06 mm which feel gritty to the touch, non-staining on the fingers and cannot be made to stick together. **Silt** is applied to particles between 0.06 and 0.002 mm which have a silky feel between the fingers and stain the hands. **Clay** is composed of particles less than 0.002 mm in size which stick together and can be polished to a smooth finish with a finger. **Loam** is a term to describe a deposit where none of the above attributes are apparent and so represents a mixture of each of the components.

139

Consistency

Once again, handling the material is the key to an accurate description under this heading. **Loose** soil crumbles very easily in the hand while **friable** deposits will stick together when pressed in the hand but can be crushed under gentle pressure from the fingers. **Compact** soils can be crushed with moderate pressure but **hard** soils need lots of effort. Finally soils which can be moulded in the hand may be recorded as **tenacious** or **sticky**. Some recording forms may ask for further information about the structure of the soil using terms such as **crumb, clod, block, prism** and **laminate** to describe the way it will naturally break into pieces.

Relationships

Those sections of the record which attempt to define the relationships between the context and the other features around it are extremely important. Without clear indications as to how the different contexts interrelate the individual cards full of information will be useless. The secret of their successful completion is in having a firm grip on the principles of stratigraphy as they apply to the site. The key terms are **above, below, adjacent to,** and **cuts** and **cut by**. 'Cuts' and 'cut' by refer to the presence of negative features such as a pit or a ditch. Any context can be cut into by a negative feature which is thus doing the cutting.

Additional elements on a recording form can include a box in which to give an indication of period, phase or date. This is normally filled in at a later date when work has started on processing the information. Sometimes it is useful to know how discrete a context was: were there clear boundaries or did it merge with surrounding deposits? On a large excavation there is a constant problem keeping track of a particular context as it becomes recorded on a welter of plans, sections and photographs. There may well be, therefore, an opportunity to list references to these additional records. Sometimes there are things that one wants to say for which none of the headings so far discussed is really adequate so there should normally be a space for additional information and comments. Finally it is important to write the name of the person who filled out the card and the date it was compiled.

Working with finds

As well as periodically stopping to collect information about an individual context there will be an on-going responsibility to record finds as they are discovered. The first question that needs to be addressed is: exactly what is a find? Unfortunately the answer to this can vary from site to site as can the policies for dealing with different categories of find. One might expect to define a find as an object, or the remains of an object, that has been manufactured by some human activity. This is a good place to start but in some cases raw materials and waste products may also be regarded as finds, as may some totally natural products like the beaver gnawed stakes found in peri-glacial deposits below the medieval mill at Bordesley Abbey. In practice there is a range of procedures based on the possible importance and significance of the evidence being gathered. For example, at an eighteenth-century forge a whole yard could be paved with slag in which case it would be recorded as a single context, with samples being taken for further analysis. At a medieval metalworking site individual lumps of slag would be kept as general finds. Their distribution might well be monitored by bagging them up according to the overlying site grid. On a prehistoric site evidence of early metalworking could be so crucial that every piece of slag would be treated as a recorded find and its position logged in three dimensions.

Even experienced diggers get something of a thrill each time a significant find is made. The important thing is to have a set of procedures clearly set out to ensure that each object receives the optimum treatment. The main principle is that once an item is unearthed the conditions which have preserved it for many hundreds or thousands of years suddenly change. It then becomes inevitable that some degree of decay or corrosion will set in immediately. The first step on making a find is, therefore, to stop and do nothing! You need to take a few seconds just to think about what comes next and above all avoid acting on impulse by wrenching the object out of the ground and capering round the site shouting 'Gold! I've found gold!' It does happen. Far more damage is caused to finds by thoughtless excavation than by leaving them where they are for a few more minutes.

Normally finds will be turned up by the edge of the trowel. Small items will then be lying loose amongst the spoil and can be carefully picked up but larger articles may well stay in ground with perhaps the bulk still buried out of sight. If you dig a hole to prize the object up you will probably end up in trouble. Apart from the risk of damaging the artefact it may well be associated with another context or find which has yet to be uncovered. The usual practice is to leave such finds in place and clean around them leaving their eventual removal to the time when the rest of the context is itself removed as part of the regular process of excavation. It can sometimes be sensible to mark such finds with a label to ensure that they are not overlooked at a later stage in the dig. The only exceptions to this might be finds of exceptional rarity or fragility in which case lifting them will almost certainly be a specialist job and you should seek help.

A certain amount of discretion needs to be observed by the digger on the subject of making finds. Not only do cries of excitement distract everyone else on site they can also suggest to any members of the public watching that valuable items are lying about on site just waiting to be picked up. For similar reasons it is important to be circumspect in discussing the day's discoveries over a glass of beer in the pub. Another temptation which should be avoided is that of cleaning any item found yourself. Apart from the possibility of damaging a fragile article you may also be removing encrusted deposits which can tell the skilled conservator much about its history.

Most digs do make a distinction between general finds and recorded finds and this affects both their handling and their recording. Most finds will be collected in a finds tray, often a strong plastic seed tray with a label attached. The label will have the coded designation for the site, the year and the context that is being dug. In addition there may be a reference to the sub-square or area you are working in. On a medieval domestic site items such as pottery fragments and animal bone would be the most common items collected. It is part of a site supervisor's responsibility to make sure that everyone knows what is to be included in the category of general finds and that everyone can actually recognize common examples of the different kinds of material coming up. These kinds of finds will frequently be recorded as a simple list, perhaps on the back of the relevant context sheet.

Important finds, which on a medieval domestic site would probably include all pieces of metalwork, will be treated as individual items with their own record. First of all they are likely to be given a number and a space on the record sheet. In this will be written the find's number, an initial identification and its position in three dimensions. A common practice is to add an additional numeral on to the basic context code so that C236/3 refers to the third recorded small find from context C236. If the find is loose it will normally be placed in an individual sealable plastic bag with one or two labels giving the full site code and the find's own reference number. The same information is written on the outside of the bag in a waterproof pen. Measuring in the location and level of the two hundredth bent iron nail can become tedious and there is sometimes a feeling that it would be better to get on with the digging. The temptation to skimp on the recording should always be resisted, subsequent plotting of spreads of old nails may reveal important evidence about a vanished timber structure. On some sites spoil is routinely sieved so that really small finds such as small flint tools, beads or bird and fish bones can be recovered.

It may be necessary to remove large amounts of a context for sampling purposes. There may be a high level of organic survival and the material will need examining by environmental scientists. After study they will be able to report on the flora and fauna from the site. Equally, samples of slag and other industrial debris may need to be sent to a metallurgist for analysis. The key principle in taking any material for scientific study is to avoid the slightest risk of contamination. This will mean working with tools specially cleaned for the purpose, carefully bagging and sealing any materials to be removed and fully labelling all samples taken. Although they rarely fall within the experience of the average digger it is worth knowing that there are also a variety of dating techniques which can be performed in the laboratory on samples removed from the site. These include radiocarbon dating which measures the time that has elapsed since a living tissue has died by measuring the amount of radioactive carbon 14 present. There is also thermoluminescence dating, which can tell how long it is since an object was last heated up by measuring the amount of light given off when it is heated today. Dendrochronology can date certain samples of timber from their patterns of growth rings.

At the end of a session all finds will be brought in off site and handed over to the finds assistants. Their job is to check that all finds are appropriately labelled and then begin a process of cleaning, recording and conserving. Volunteers are often asked to take on this role either as a full-time job or as a break from labouring on site. The first stage will normally be to wash the more robust finds, especially examples of pottery, tile and bone. Despite their apparent toughness all finds need gentle and intelligent handling. A muddy chunk of pottery may have deposits on the inner surfaces giving evidence of use; or an unpromising lump of bone may have marks of butchery or even a carved design. Things like this come up regularly during finds washing and there should be a finds supervisor to whom you can refer unusual developments.

Washing is normally done in plastic bowls using clean water. Once the item has been immersed in water for a moment or two the fingers can begin to gently massage away the adhering soil. Brushes of varying degrees of hardness and size, ranging from a scrubbing brush to a tooth brush, will be available. Care must be taken when using a brush to avoid marking the surface of the find by over vigorous scrubbing. Even apparently solid materials like pottery can become quite soft in water and so easily marked. Only one item at a time should be washed. It is not a good idea to tip the whole lot into the bowl together, finds can

84 Washing and labelling finds.

get broken or abraded by this kind of treatment (84).

Once the finds have been washed they are left to dry before a decision is made as to their fate. The director and site supervisor will regularly inspect the washed finds. This will give them a better idea of the kind of things coming out from a particular context and may result in some alterations being made to the records. The director will also decide what will be kept and what thrown away. Some items such as curiously shaped natural stones may not be any kind of find at all. From the digger's point of view it is always better to keep dubious items, it is easy enough to throw them away after they have been checked. If there are large quantities of certain kinds of find, broken roof tiles for example, they will probably be sorted, counted and weighed according to type and then thrown away apart from a few which are kept as representatives of the different categories identified (85).

Those items which are kept will next need further labelling. Many finds can be marked by writing directly on to the surface in waterproof black ink. Sometimes a white roundel will be painted on to dark objects before they are labelled. Very small items or finds with a decorated surface will have small labels tied to them or be inserted into labelled bags or boxes. Further information may be added to the code number at this point as there may be a separate numbering system for recorded small finds. This will probably be pre-fixed with a letter code indicating

the kind of material it is and will tie in with an additional set of object record cards. On sites where a sizeable proportion of one kind of find is likely to come up there may well be separate arrangements and a special recording system to cope with items like architectural fragments or waterlogged wood.

Many finds will need some kind of emergency first-aid to prevent further serious deterioration in their condition. The basic principle is to store items in an environment which resembles as closely as possible the surroundings from which they were removed. This would mean keeping pieces of worked leather from the filling of a well in water in plastic tubs. Iron objects from dry sandy soil would sit happily in stout cardboard boxes with silica gel to keep them free from moisture. For those objects which require immediate treatment a variety of unpleasant chemicals may be kept to hand but this really is work for the specialist.

85 Inside the finds hut, record cards and materials for packing.

On-site survey

Back on site the digger could well be called on to help with other bits of recording, including survey work and photography. We have already looked in Chapter 3 at simple survey techniques as applied to earthworks and buildings and the basic principles remain unchanged. Surveying by

145

offsets and triangulation both play an important part in drawing up plans of excavated features. A local grid which covers the entire site will have been established at an early stage in the excavation. This will be marked out, usually with white painted posts, round the periphery of the dig. It will in turn be linked to a series of fixed points which can be returned to year after year. The local grid may be further linked into the national grid. Whatever survey method is actually used it will have to tie into the basic grid.

On site a number of drawings will need to be prepared. This could mean drawing each individual pebble on a surface many metres across, plotting subtle changes in colour and texture in the area around a hearth or planning the twisted remains of a collapsed wooden fence. The normal practice is to use a planning frame. This device consists of a rigid frame, 1 m square, with string across it at intervals of 10 or 20 cm marking out a grid. This is laid on to the surface that is to be drawn at a known location fixed from the site grid. The details of that surface are then drawn in by eye, working directly on to squared paper, normally at a scale of 1 to 20. A 20 cm square on the ground will thus appear as a 1 cm square on the paper. Occasionally a hand-tape may be used to check the sizes of individual objects but with practice much of the work can be done by eye (86).

On a large site a number of these frames may be in use at any one time. This is back-breaking work which tests the patience. Up to 50,000 individual items may have to be drawn on a simple 10 m (33 ft) square!

86　A drawing frame levelled in place and ready to use.

You will be likely to have a drawing board balanced on one leg while you crane forward to ensure that you are getting a truly vertical view down on to the surface you are drawing. The sun may be blazing on your neck or the rain trickling down it but you still have an obligation to work as methodically and accurately as you can. Despite this most people do enjoy drawing and there is satisfaction to be derived from completing the work. The final plan will be traced after individual pieces of work have been checked and then taped together to form a mosaic view.

Most drawing on site will be done with a hard pencil, 6H, on plastic drawing film. Clear sheets of this will be taped on to a drawing board over a large sheet of graph paper enabling the basic outline of the site grid to be drawn directly. Each excavation will have its own set of conventions. Hachures will be used to show changes in slope. The boundary between two different contexts will be shown as a continuous line whilst a broken line will be used where the edge is uncertain. Charcoal, building stone, tile, bone and wood may all have their own distinctive patterns of shading. Some information, about finds for example, may be written on to the plan. All the contexts which are drawn should be clearly labelled with their number. The plan should also carry the full name of the site and the year, the scale, an arrow showing north, the date of the drawing and the names of those responsible. Finally each drawing will have its own unique number for reference.

Because drawing is so demanding in time and effort the question is often asked, 'Why do we bother to draw things at all?' It is a good question, especially now that there are so many sophisticated methods of recording a site photographically. It may well be that the kind of expensive equipment needed is just not available but there is another more positive reason for choosing to draw. In order to draw one is forced into prolonged close study of the area which can reveal patterns and features a more cursory glance would miss. Drawing is also a selective process, decisions about what to put in and what to leave out are a form of interpretation which confronts the archaeologist with some of the conclusions he or she has already reached about the site.

Both the sides of the excavated area and temporary strips left across it give a vertical view down through the site. These sections also have to be drawn and the method is similar to the one we noted in Chapter 3 for drawing earthwork profiles. The job really demands two people. As the excavation has proceeded care will have been taken to leave these faces as clean and as near vertical as possible. The section will be straightened and then cleaned and perhaps sprayed with a fine mist to freshen up the colours. The next step is to fasten a section line against the face to be drawn, using good quality builder's line and a couple of nails. This line must be level so either a line level or an optical level and staff are used to ensure this is so and to determine the position of the line with reference to site datum. A 10 or 20 m tape is then stretched along the line and held in place with clips. The person who is to do the actual drawing will then sit down so that he or she has a good overall view without being too far away to miss the detail. The second member of the team, armed with a hand tape, will work along the line measuring the position of significant points as they are called for. If the boundary between two layers is clear the helper may proceed to take measurements vertically from the line every 50 cm. If special features are observed then the measurements can be given at closer intervals. Sometimes, where the section is a deep one, it may be necessary to use a plumb bob to ensure that the measurements are truly vertical. Meanwhile the person back at the drawing board will be plotting the measured points on to the scale drawing and putting in any further detail by eye. Acting as the measurer is often the beginner's first introduction to drawing on site. It is all much more fun than it sounds (87).

87 Drawing a stone-by-stone wall elevation, the method is same as is used for section drawing.

Work on a cumulative section based on temporary baulks is a little more demanding and requires effective organization. The great advantage with this kind of recording is that a vertical view can be produced across any part of the site. Each time a new layer is exposed a section line is strung up and tapes used to draw its profile. The layer is then removed up to the baulk so that it can be drawn in section before it is completely removed. Once another layer is uncovered the whole process is repeated. Section drawings, like plans, need to be labelled with information as to their location, content and origin (**88**).

88 Section drawing, through the robbing trench on the north aisle, Bordesley Abbey.

Photography

The photographic record is another key element in building up a picture of the development of a site. In many ways it complements the drawn record, being strong on objectivity yet short on explanation. Many archaeologists pride themselves on their photographic skills and use some very expensive equipment to get excellent results. Most excavations will use several cameras. There will probably be a large-format single lens reflex (SLR) camera to take high quality black-and-white prints for publication, a couple of 35 mm single lens reflex cameras,

149

one for colour prints and one for slides and perhaps a Polaroid camera for instant record shots. Most of us have to content ourselves with a more modest set up as described in Chapter 1. The wide-angle lens can be used to picture the whole site and may also have a macro facility for close-ups of individual finds while the zoom lens can be used for more limited areas and specific features. The ability to view and frame the shot before releasing the shutter is an important one when you are trying to bring out some of the special subtleties of the excavated surface and the light has to be just right. To this end a tripod is essential and you may have to wait for some time before the right combination of light and shade comes along.

A high standard of cleanliness is always important on site but once the time for photography arrives near impossible demands are made on the workforce's skill and patience! The basic cleaning will involve a very light scraping or brushing of the surface to remove all stray particles of dirt, sections will be tidied up, all lines, tapes and tools removed and, if it is to appear in the picture, the perimeter of site sorted out too. The director will, of course, want everything to look its best primarily so that the archaeological features show up as well as possible for the record. It is also the case that the photographs are likely to be most people's only contact with the site and there is an understandable tendency to link a scruffy site with scrappy digging.

Apart from certain special techniques, most archaeological photography uses natural light. A reasonably diffuse yet fairly strong light, as seen on a cloudy summer day, is ideal for most sites. Low levels of illumination lead to long exposure times but are not as troublesome as bright sunlight which casts strong shadows thus obscuring much detail as well as bouncing back up off the surface producing glare. This can be removed with filters but the results are often flat and disappointing. On many photographs it is crucial to get as great a depth of field as possible so that points all across the picture are sharply in focus. This is achieved by closing down the aperture and lengthening the exposure time.

On site once the final cleaning has been completed a scale will be introduced into the shot. For close up work this may be a short 30 cm scale painted black and white to mark the divisions, on wider views a 2 m ranging rod is commonly used. Some directors like to use a notice board with plug in or magnetic letters to label the view with the site code, context number and date. Colour monitor cards may also be included as well as a pointer to indicate north. When everything is ready it may be necessary to give the area a final spray to brighten up the colours before the picture is taken (89).

Different view points can bring out different features of a site. A low level or oblique shot will underline the vertical undulations of the surface while a vertical view will show features like post-holes in their true spatial arrangement. Where an overall picture is required people will spend a lot of time and effort trying for extra height. We have already noted some of the techniques available for aerial photography but most people will also want to be a little nearer the ground with a stable platform to work from. The roof of an adjacent building or even a conveniently parked mini-bus can be useful but in their absence most digs invest in the kind of lightweight aluminium scaffolding tower used by the decorating trade. They can lift the photographer anything up to 10 m (33 ft) into the air but they can be unstable. If you want to use one that is on site check that it is on a secure and level base, that it is tied down with guy ropes, and that only one person at a time is up it.

Vertical photographs are not only useful to give a general view of the site; they can also form the basis for making detailed drawings. We have already explored some simple photogrammetric methods and the same ideas can be applied to an excavated surface. Pairs of stereoscopic photographs can be used to draw out a three dimensional map of the excavated features. Although it takes a little while to set up once in

89 Spraying the site prior to photographing it.

151

90 Philip Rahtz
photographed
photographing a
timber sluice gate.

91 Site photography,
the Saxon chapel at
Guiting Power
(copyright reserved Dr
A.J. Marshall).

place this method can cover the ground very quickly; unfortunately the equipment can be expensive and the follow up costly and time consuming.

There are a few archaeologists who have made their entry into the subject through their interest in photography and it is certainly an area where a particularly knowledgeable or talented amateur can make themselves indispensable on site. Similarly computers are becoming common fixtures on many excavations because of the large quantities of information generated. Many professional archaeologists feel perfectly at home with new technology, but there are plenty who feel that they have enough to do on site and who may welcome someone with a computing background on to the staff. Excavation is a group undertaking to which everyone has something to contribute, whether it be simply muscle or some particular technical knowledge or expertise; the important thing is to find out what is going on and get involved!

92 The next generation: 10 and 11 year olds survey the site of a deserted medieval village on Exmoor.

Useful addresses

Archaeology Abroad
31–34 Gordon Square
London WC1H 0PY
Association for Industrial Archaeology
c/o Ironbridge Gorge Museum
The Wharfage
Ironbridge
Telford TF8 7AW

British Archaeological Association
D.W. MacDowell
Admont
Dancers End
Tring
Herts HP28 6JY
British Association for Local History
Shopwyke Hall
Chichester PO20 6BQ
British Museum Society
c/o The British Museum
Great Russell Street
London WC1B 3DG

CADW
Brunel House
2 Fitzalen Place
Newport Road
Cardiff CF2 1UY
Cambrian Archaeological Association
Richard Kelly
52 Upper Garth Road
Bangor
Gwynedd LL57 2SS
Council for British Archaeology (CBA)
112 Kennington Road
London S11 6RE

Council for Independent Archaeology
Mike Rumbold
3 West Street
Weedon Bec
Northampton NN7 4QU
Council for Scottish Archaeology
c/o Royal Museum of Scotland
York Buildings
1 Queen Street
Edinburgh EH1 2JD
Current Archaeology
9 Nassington Road
London NW3 2TX

English Heritage (Headquarters)
Fortress House
23 Savile Row
London W1X 1AB
English Heritage – Education Service
15–17 Great Marlborough Street
London W1V 1AF
English Heritage – Membership Department
PO Box 1BB
London W1A 1BB
English Heritage – Postal Sales
PO Box 299
Northampton NN6 9RY

Historic Buildings and Monuments (Scotland)
20 Brandon Street
Edinburgh EH3 5RA

Institute of Field Archaeologists
c/o Birmingham University
Box 363
Birmingham B15 2TT

Medieval Settlement Research Group
c/o Department of Geography
Downing Place
Cambridge CB2 3EN

National Farmers Union
Agriculture House
Knightsbridge
London SW1X 7NJ

National Museum of Scotland
Chambers Street
Edinburgh EH1 1JF

National Museum of Wales
Cathays Park
Cardiff CF1 6LB

National Trust
36 Queen Annes Gate
London SW1H 9AS

Prehistoric Society
c/o The Museum Bookshop
36 Great Russell Street
London WC1B 3PP

Royal Archaeological Institute
c/o Society of Antiquaries
Burlington House
Piccadilly
London W1V 0HS

Royal Commission on the Historical Monuments of England
Fortress House
23 Savile Row
London W1X 2JQ

Royal Commission on the Historical Monuments of England – Air Photography and Threatened Buildings Sections
Alexander House
19 Fleming Way
Swindon SN1 2NQ

Royal Commission on Ancient and Historic Monuments (Scotland)
52–54 Melville Street

Edinburgh EH3 7HF

Royal Commission on Ancient and Historic Monuments in Wales
Crown Building
Plas Crug
Aberystwyth
Dyfed SY23 2HP

Society of Antiquaries of Scotland
c/o Royal Museum of Scotland
Queen Street
Edinburgh EH2 1JD

Society for Medieval Archaeology
Alan Vince
CLAU – The Lawn
Union Road
Lincoln LN1 3BL

Society for Post-Medieval Archaeology
Philomena Jackson
13 Sommerville Road
Bishopston
Bristol BS7 9AD

Society for the Promotion of Roman Studies
Institute of Archaeology
31–34 Gordon Square
London WC1H 0PY

Ulster Archaeological Society
c/o Department of Archaeology
Elmwood Avenue
Belfast BT7 1NN

Vernacular Architecture Group
N.W. Alcock
Brick Field
20 Kiln Lane
Betchworth
Surrey RH3 7LX

Young Archaeologists Club
Karen McMahon
Clifford Chambers
4 Clifford Street
York YO1 1RD

Further reading

(Books that, at the time of writing, are out of print are marked with an asterisk.)

B.T. Batsford Ltd – 4 Fitzhardinge Street, London, W1H 0AH
Batsford has the largest list of full length archaeological books with a strong interest in practical techniques and links with local history. The following are a selection that are useful as a beginning:

Aston, M. *Interpreting the Landscape: Landscape Archaeology and Local History* (Reprint) 0 7134 3650 6
Barker, P. *Techniques of Archaeological Excavation* 0 7134 2739 6
Brown, A. *Fieldwork for Archaeologists and Local Historians* 0 7134 4842 3
Carver, M. *Underneath English Towns: Interpreting Urban Archaeology* 0 7134 3638 7
Clark, A. *Seeing Beneath the Soil: Prospecting Methods in Archaeology* 0 7134 5859 3
Fleming, A. *The Dartmoor Reaves: An Archaeological Investigation* 0 7134 5666 3
Greene, K. *Archaeology: An Introduction* 0 7134 3648 8
Riden, P. *Local History: A Handbook for Beginners* 0 7134 3871 1
Smith, L. *Investigating Old Buildings* 0 7134 3534 4
*Taylor, C. *Fieldwork in Medieval Archaeology* 0 7134 2872 4

Batsford/English Heritage
This new series concentrates mainly on individual monuments and uses archaeological discoveries, both from excavation and fieldwork to describe them in their historical and landscape setting.

Bédoyère, G. de la *Roman Towns in Britain*
Beresford, M. & Hurst, J. *Wharram Percy: Deserted Medieval Village*
Clark, C. *Ironbridge Gorge*
Coppack, G. *Abbeys and Priories*
Johnson, S. *Hadrian's Wall*
Malone, C. *Avebury*
McNeill, T. *Castles*
Parker-Pearson, M. *Bronze Age Britain*
Parnell, G. *The Tower of London* (forthcoming)
Pryor, F. *Flag Fen: Prehistoric Fenland Centre*
Richards, J. *Stonehenge*
Richards, J. D. *Viking Age England*
Rodwell, W. *Church Archaeology*
Sharples, N. *Maiden Castle*
Welch, M. *Anglo-Saxon England*
Woodward, A. *Shrines and Sacrifice*

Basil Blackwell – 108 Cowley Road, Oxford, OX4 1JF

Rahtz, P. *Invitation to Archaeology* 0 631 14107 3
(An 'insider's' book which attempts to tell the truth about what archaeologists are really up to, at least as far as one eminent practitioner is concerned.)

British Museum Publications – 46 Bloomsbury Street, London WC1B 3QQ
The British Museum publishes a large number of archaeology books mainly relating to objects in their collections.

Cherry, C. and Longworth, I. (Eds.) *Archaeology in Britain since 1945* 0 7141 2035 9
(The best summary of the discoveries made by modern British archaeology.)

Collins – 8 Grafton Street, London, W1X 3LA
*Wood, E.S. *Collins Field Guide to Archaeology in Britain* 0 0021 9235 7
(A wonderfully comprehensive guide to archaeological features in the landscape but sadly short of illustrations.)

Council for British Archaeology –
112 Kennington Road, London SE11 6RE
The CBA publish many of the standard guides to practical archaeology as well as a number of research reports on general matters and specific sites.

Practical Handbooks:
1 – *Recording Worked Stone* 0 906780 71 3
2 – *Survey by Prismatic Compass*, Farrar 0 906780 72 1
3 – *British Archaeology: an introductory booklist*, Dyer 0 906780 70 5
4 – *British Archaeological Thesaurus*, Lavell 0 906780 77 2
5 – *Recording Timber Framed Buildings*, Alcock *et al* 0 906780 73 X
6 – *Safety in Archaeological Fieldwork*, Olivier 0 906780 80 2
7 – *Recording a Church: an illustrated glossary*, Cocke *et al* 0 906780 84 5
8 – *Churches and Chapels: recording places of worship*, Parsons 0 906780 86 1
9 – *Talking Archaeology: a handbook for lecturer and organisers*, Adkins, L. and Adkins, R.A. 0 906780 87 X
10 – *Recording Medieval Floor Tiles*, Stopford, J. 1 872414 03 6
Binns, G. and Corbishley, M. and Halkon, P. *The Archaeological Resource Book* 1 872414 18 4
Binns, G. and Gardiner, J. *Guide to University Undergraduate Courses in Archaeology* 1 872414 14 1

Boulton, P. *Signposts to Archaeological Publication*, 3rd ed. 1991 1 872414 04 4
Jones, J. *How to Record Graveyards* 0 906780 43 8

A number of standard record cards and forms are also available from the C.B.A.

David and Charles – Brunel House, Forde Road, Newton Abbott, Devon, TQ12 4PU
David and Charles have a long tradition of publishing topographical and historical material, some of it often of very specialist interest.

*Aston, M. and Rowley, R. *Landscape Archaeology* 0 7153 6670 X

Faber and Faber – 3 Queen Square, London, WC1N 3AU
Faber and Faber publish some architectural material including a number of important titles on historic houses.

Brunskill, R.W. *Illustrated Handbook of Vernacular Architecture* 0 5711 1124 7
*Dyer, J. *Southern England: an Archaeological Guide* 0 5711 0317 0
*Houlder, C. *Wales: an Archaeological Guide* 0 5710 8221 1
*MacKie, E.W. *Scotland: an Archaeological Guide* 0 5710 9871 1

HMSO – St Crispins, Duke Street, Norwich, NR3 1PD
As well as publishing many important specialist and general books on archaeology HMSO are also responsible for producing the inventories of historic monuments drawn up by the Royal Commissions.

Buchanan, T. *Photographing Historic Buildings* 0 11 701123 1
Binks, G., Dyke, J. and Dagnall, P. *Visitors Welcome – A manual on the presentation and interpretation of archaeological excavations* 0 11 701210 6

Shire Publications Ltd – Cromwell House, Church Street, Princes Risborough, Aylesbury, Bucks, HP17 9AJ
Shire have published large numbers of slim

paperback volumes on a whole range of archaeological, architectural and historical topics in a variety of different series.

Shire Archaeology has over 50 titles some on specific classes of site such as:

Burl, A. *Prehistoric Stone Circles*
Dyer, J. *Hillforts of England and Wales*
Taylor, C. *Archaeology of Gardens*
Wilson, D. *Moated Sites*

Then there are volumes on particular groups of finds:
Casey, P.J. *Roman Coinage in Britain*
Draper, J. *Post-medieval Pottery*
Lang, J. *Anglo-Saxon Sculpture*
Taylor, M. *Wood in Archaeology*

And finally books on techniques:
Dyer, J. *Teaching Archaeology in Schools*
Lock, G. & Wilcock, J. *Computer Archaeology*

Shire Albums examine a range of industrial, agricultural and domestic subjects such as *Clay Tobacco Pipes, Ironworking, Dairying Bygones, Old Farm Tools, Needlework Tools* and *Writing Antiques.*

The **Discovering**... series has covered a huge range of historical and topographical subjects including a series of regional archaeological guides, now out of print. Other relevant titles include:

Bodey, H. *Discovering Industrial Archaeology and History*

Harris, R. *Discovering Timber Framed Buildings*
Iredale, D. *Discovering Your Old House*
Kinross, J. *Discovering Battlefields of England*
Kinross, J. *Discovering Castles in England and Wales*

Ravette Books – 3 Glenside Estate, Star Road, Partridge Green, Horsham, West Sussex, RH13 8RA

Bahn, P. *Bluff Your Way in Archaeology*
1 85304 102 5
(An entertaining look at archaeologists and their odd ways.)

Thames and Hudson – 30 Bloomsbury Street, London WC1B 3QP
As publishers of many books on art history Thames and Hudson often cross into archaeological territory especially in their series on ancient peoples and places.

Bahn, P. and Renfrew, C. *Archaeology – Theories, Methods and Practice* 0 500 276056

Walker Books – 87 Vauxhall Walk, London SE11 5HJ

Eccles, C. *The Rose Theatre* 1 85459 076 6
(The gripping story of the recent controversy surrounding the excavation of the site and as such one of the few accounts of the inter-relationship between archaeology, politics and public opinion.)

Index

INDEX